MOZAMBICAN CIVIL WAR

MARXIST–APARTHEID PROXY, 1977–1992

STEPHEN EMERSON

Pen & Sword
MILITARY

First published in Great Britain in 2019 by
PEN AND SWORD MILITARY
an imprint of
Pen and Sword Books Ltd
47 Church Street
Barnsley
South Yorkshire S70 2AS

ISBN 978 1 52672 849 4

Maps by George Anderson
Front cover photo courtesy of Centro de Formação Fotografica, Maputo, Mozambique
Back cover photo courtesy of André Thomashausen
Typeset by Aura Technology and Software Services, India
Printed and bound by CPI Group (UK) Ltd, Croydon, CR0 4YY

Pen & Sword Books Ltd incorporates the imprints of Pen & Sword
Archaeology, Atlas, Aviation, Battleground, Discovery, Family History, History, Maritime, Military,
Naval, Politics, Railways, Select, Social History, Transport, True Crime, Claymore Press, Frontline
Books, Leo Cooper, Praetorian Press, Remember When, Seaforth Publishing and Wharncliffe.

For a complete list of Pen and Sword titles please contact
Pen and Sword Books Limited
47 Church Street, Barnsley, South Yorkshire, S70 2AS, England
email: enquiries@pen-and-sword.co.uk
website: www.pen-and-sword.co.uk

CONTENTS

LIST OF MAPS

GLOSSARY

AFZ	Air Force of Zimbabwe
ANC	African National Congress (South Africa)
bandidos armados	armed bandits; Frelimo name for Renamo guerrillas
Beira corridor	rail and road network, plus oil pipeline running across central Mozambique from Beira to Mutare (Zimbabwe)
BMATT	British Military Advisory Training Team
CIA	Central Intelligence Agency (United States)
CIO	Central Intelligence Organization (Rhodesia/ Zimbabwe)
ComOps	Combined Operations Headquarters (Rhodesia)
Dak	C-47 "Dakota" transport aircraft
DST	Directorate of Special Tasks (South Africa)
DZ	drop zone for men and matériel by parachute
FADM	*Forças Armadas de Defesa Moçambique* (Mozambique Defense Armed Forces), 1992–present
FAM	*Forças Armadas de Moçambique* (Armed Forces of Mozambique), 1982–1991
flechas	members of the special Portuguese commando unit under PIDE control; operated in Angola and Mozambique (lit. "arrows")
FPLM	*Forças Populares de Libertacão de Moçambique* (Popular Forces for the Liberation of Mozambique), Frelimo's armed wing, 1975–1981
Frelimo	*Frente de Libertação de Moçambique* (Front for the Liberation of Mozambique), FPLM's political wing
Gersony Report	U.S. government-funded study on Mozambican violence published in April 1988; Renamo blamed for majority of violence against civilians
GPA	General Peace Agreement; signed in Rome in October 1992
Hercules	C-130 transport aircraft
JVC	Joint Verification Commission
Limpopo corridor	rail and road network roughly paralleling the Limpopo River and running from Maputo to Chicualacuala in southeast Zimbabwe
MNR	Mozambique National Resistance; early Rhodesian name for Renamo
Nkomati Accord	non-aggression pact signed between South Africa and Mozambique in March 1984

Operation Altar	South African covert assistance to Renamo, March 1980–January 1983; renamed Operation Mila after January 1983
Operation Bumper	Rhodesian military assistance to Renamo
Operation Cob Web	Zimbabwean escort operations along the Tete corridor
Operation Lifeline	Zimbabwean defense of the Beira corridor
Operation Open Way	Zimbabwean defense of the Limpopo corridor
PIDE	*Polícia Internacional e de Defesa do Estado*, International Police for the Defence of the State (Lisbon's equivalent of the secret police)
recces	South African reconnaissance commandos
Red Berets	Mozambican commando unit
Renamo	*Resistência Nacional Moçambicana* (Mozambican National Resistance)
RLI	Rhodesian Light Infantry
RPG-7	Soviet-made rocket-propelled grenade launcher
SADCC	Southern Africa Development Coordination Conference
SAAF	South African Air Force
SADF	South African Defence Force
SAS	Special Air Service (Rhodesia/ Zimbabwe)
STF	Special Task Force (Zimbabwe)
stop group	prepositioned troops placed in a blocking position
Sunray	military voice procedure codename for local commander
TPDF	Tanzanian People's Defence Force
Voz da Africa Livre	Voice of Free Africa; Renamo radio station
ZANLA	Zimbabwe African National Liberation Army; ZANU's armed wing
ZANU	Zimbabwe African National Union
ZAPU	Zimbabwe African People's Union
ZIPRA	Zimbabwe People's Revolutionary Army; ZAPU's armed wing
ZNA	Zimbabwe National Army

Mozambique.

1. THE COLD WAR IN AFRICA

Though not preordained to such a fate, the march of history in the post-World War II period would dramatically transform the heretofore neglected African continent into a major venue for superpower competition and military confrontation during the Cold War. As such the continent and its people would find themselves caught up in a global ideological struggle between the United States and the Soviet Union not of their own making. Nonetheless, they would find themselves forced to cope with an intense level of sustained violence throughout the last half of the 20th century as the impact of the Cold War played out across Africa.

The superpower competition to acquire new allies, gain influence, and secure access to strategic minerals in Africa often played out along diplomatic and economic lines, but where the stakes were the highest—in places like Egypt, the Congo, the Horn of Africa or southern Africa—the military tool of engagement dominated both Washington's and Moscow's thinking. But rather than confront each other directly, each side sought to shore up their African allies by rewarding them with generous military aid packages or conversely undermining hostile regimes by providing covert military assistance and training to anti-government rebels. The latter tactic led to rise, and extensive use, of proxy armies by the superpowers or their regional allies, which often inflamed longstanding regional tensions, chronic societal and political divisions or helped to sustain high levels of civil conflict.

The Wind of Change Sweeps across Africa

The collapse of the old order in Europe and the devastation wrought by the Second World War signaled the death knell for colonial empires in Africa and triggered a wave of independence beginning in the mid-1950s. For the most part, Africa's old colonial rulers recognized the anachronist nature of colonialism in the new post-war world and their inability to politically and economically justify its continuation. A few, however, still clung to their visions of empire and grandeur and would bitterly resist the rising tide African nationalism. Thus, while much of colonial Africa experienced a relatively peaceful transition to independence, parts of the continent would become caught up in violent struggles that would last for many years. Not surprisingly, these struggles by their very nature tended to align along the East–West divide with the African forces of self-determination and change aligning with the revolutionary ideology of communism and anti-imperialism against the status quo ante of stability and Western capitalism.

Early on the Soviet Union and the People's Republic of China sought to exploit this situation by providing diplomatic, economic, and military assistance (including guerrilla training) to nascent African nationalist insurgencies. In contrast the United

Portuguese Prime Minister Marcelo Caetano. (File photo)

States found itself aligning with European colonial powers—often at the expense of moderate nationalists—in the name of stemming the advance of global communism into Africa. Broader geopolitical considerations in the case of Portugal—a NATO member granting U.S. access to its bases in the Azores Islands—would also come into play as a way for Washington to rationalize its stance on the continuation of Portuguese colonialism. In what would become the ultimate litmus test of the Cold War, African

President Gerald Ford and First Secretary Leonid Brezhnev share a cordial moment in 1974 just as the Cold War in Africa is about to heat up.

Portuguese troops embark at Lisbon for duty in Africa. (Photo courtesy Al J. Venter)

By the early 1970s Lisbon was struggling under the financial and psychological burden of having to fight three African insurgencies simultaneously.

Holden Roberto's National Front for the Liberation of Angola (FNLA) was the largest of the three liberation movement fighting against the Portuguese, but it often proved to be the least effective guerrilla force.

independence movements and emergent African governments were forced to declare their allegiance to one side or the other. Thus, the ever-present specter of superpower

competition was constantly overshadowing domestic considerations in the creation and evolution of modern-day Africa.

Beginning with the escalating violence of the Algerian civil war in 1954–1962 as France sought to maintain its historical and political grip on its North African territory, and Ghana's peaceful transition in 1957, through the chaos following the collapse of Belgian rule in central Africa in the 1960s to uneventful handovers of power in Zambia and Botswana, African colonies and protectorates steadily gained their independence. By 1970, more than 35 new countries had come into existence on the continent and nearly all were being courted by either the United States or

Dr. Eduardo Mondlane, the founding father of Frelimo, would be assassinated by Portuguese agents in Dar es Salaam, Tanzania on February 3, 1969 and succeeded by Frelimo's military commander, Samora Machel.

the Soviet Union as the great geopolitical game in Africa began to play out. Using the promise of generous economic aid, subsidized military equipment sales, and relying on teams of technical experts and military advisers, both Washington and Moscow sought to build and burnish competing blocs of local allies in what was becoming a new scramble for Africa. Importantly, the superpowers increasingly viewed their competition in zero-sum terms—one's gain was the other's loss—which enormously increased the stakes for both sides.

Unable to match Western economic largess, however, Moscow increasingly sought to make common cause with progressive regimes and revolutionary leaders, like Kwame Nkrumah of Ghana, Sékou Touré of Guinea, Angola's Aghostino Neto, and Patrice Lumumba from the former Belgian Congo, and assist in the political development of tightly controlled Marxist parties. This not only facilitated long-term ideological and doctrinal ties to Moscow, but created a ready-made platform for projecting pro-Soviet power and influence throughout the continent. But it was in area of military engagement through the provision of arms, training, and advisers that Moscow staked its claim, providing some $700 million in military weaponry in the first two decades of African independence.[1] This allowed the Soviets to leverage their influence with nationalist insurgent movements before independence or to help sustain revolutionary governments once they came to power. The critical role of Soviet military aid became even more telling as the 1970s dawned and the East–West conflict began to heat up in various parts of the continent.

Portugal's African Colonial Wars

By the early 1960s the Portuguese government of Prime Minister Antonio Salazar found itself facing a monumental watershed as fervent political demands for self-determination and independence within its African colonies threatened to uproot Lisbon's imperialist dream and relegate the country once again to the backwaters of Western Europe. First in Angola and then in Guinea-Bissau and Cape Verde, and finally in Mozambique, African nationalist movements had taken up the armed struggle for independence. Rather than attempt to seek some form of political accommodation to assuage nationalists' demands, the authoritarian Salazar government opted to militarily crush the rebellions and ensure the continuation of Portuguese rule at any price. Ultimately, however, the economic and psychological burden of fighting three full-blown counterinsurgencies across the length and width of Africa would prove too much, leading to the implosion of the Portuguese state in April 1974.

Angola
Following a protracted period of urban unrest that resulted in harsh crackdowns by Portuguese colonial authorities, the armed struggle was launched in the north

of the country in early 1961. The attacks targeted the Portuguese settler community and created a pattern of attack and reprisal that would set a bitter tone for the coming conflict. To cope with the deteriorating security situation, Lisbon would increase its military presence from 3,000 to 50,000 men by the end of the year. While the Portuguese struggled to transform their conventional and conscript military into an effective counterinsurgency force, division and dissension wracked the nationalist movements. This led to the formation by the mid-1960s of three independent and competing guerrilla forces: The National Front for the Liberation of Angola (FLNA), which was numerically the largest of the anti-Portuguese forces during the war; the Soviet-supported Popular Movement for the Liberation of Angola (MPLA); and the smaller, Chinese-backed National Union for the Total Independence of Angola (UNITA). Often pre-occupied with burnishing their own international image or undercutting rivals, none of the three guerrilla forces posed a significant threat to the Portuguese, who were content to cede much of the remote countryside to the insurgents while continuing to secure the cities and vital economic regions. The ensuing low-intensity conflict—with little more than 100 Portuguese deaths per year—largely stalemated along these lines up until the April 25, 1974 coup in Lisbon. And with no clear preeminent nationalist movement arising from the anti-colonial struggle, it would set the stage for the coming civil war in 1975.

Guinea-Bissau
In sharp contrast to Angola, the African Independence Party for the Independence of Guinea and Cabo Verde (PAIGC) under the leadership of Amilcar Cabral dominated the armed struggle from its beginning in January 1963 and proved extremely effective at ousting the Portuguese from the south of the country early on. Moreover, despite the presence of more than 30,000 men, the colonial government was unable to reverse the tide, forcing it into a defensive posture for the duration of the war. Somewhat surprisingly, Guinea-Bissau witnessed some of the heaviest fightng of the colonial wars, with the Portuguese relying heavily on air bombardment (including the use of napalm) to counter new PAIGC advances and launch strikes deep into guerrilla-controlled territory. The arrival of Brigadier Antonio de Spinola in late 1968 failed to reverse the situation despite his civic action and hearts and minds programs that were designed to weaken the nationalists' appeal. The acquisition of heavy weapons, including artillery and surface-to-air missiles, by the PAIGC in 1970 accelerated Portuguese losses in both men and territory and an ill-advised cross-border strike against guerrilla bases in neighboring Guinea ended in a complete military and diplomatic disaster. At the time of the Lisbon coup the Portuguese army was just barely holding on.

Mozambique

The armed struggle only commenced in 1964 and in the very far north of the country and posed little threat to Portuguese rule. Moreover, secret police (PIDE) crackdowns in the larger urban areas devastated nationalist infrastructure in the central and southern parts of the country. Like in Angola, competing political ideologies, ethnic suspicions and rivalries, and personal ambitions divided the nationalist movement in Mozambique and undermined the guerrillas' effectiveness. It was only through the forceful intervention of other African nationalist leaders that led to the formation of the Front for the Liberation of Mozambique (Frelimo). Nevertheless, defections and internal dissent would plague Frelimo throughout the war and even result in the assassination of its founding leader, Eduardo Mondlane, in 1969. The presence of more than 40,000 Portuguese troops and several large-scale offensives, however, failed to stem Frelimo's advances southward. By 1972 the guerrilla army had crossed the Zambezi River into the center of the country and was poised to threaten the country's second largest city, Beira, in early 1974.

The legacy of Portugal's colonial conflicts would have significant repercussions, particularly for Angola and Mozambique, throughout the remainder of the Cold War in Africa. For while the ending of Portuguese rule in 1975 brought about the advent of African independence to these countries, it did not bring an end to the strife and division that plagued multiple and competing nationalist movements and personalities. Moreover, the relatively small size of the liberated zones, the geographically confided war zones, and the often narrow ethnic and racial makeup of the guerrilla leadership in Angola and Mozambique significantly hamstrung efforts to create a truly nationwide independence movement with broad appeal. Thus, the imposition of one-party rule following independence often fueled resistance and hostility to the new governments, creating a ready-made opportunity for external forces to exploit. And exploit them they would.

Battleground Southern Africa

For the entrenched white minority regimes of southern Africa the day of reckoning was fast approaching as the final wave of independence came crashing down upon them. With the battle lines drawn at the Zambezi River, the fate of Portuguese colonies of Angola and Mozambique, as well as the embattled settler societies in Rhodesia, South West Africa, and South Africa would be decided. This would become the penultimate test for the superpowers. The forces of African nationalism and international communism would be pitted against pro-Western governments that viewed themselves as the last bastion of Western civilization, often in the guise of Christianity, in a series of deadly proxy wars that would rock the region for decades, producing mass suffering, and destruction on a scale rarely seen.

Surprisingly it would not be in the rarified air of the White House or the Kremlin that would set in motion the play of events, but on the streets of Lisbon when the Portuguese government of Marcelo Caetano was overthrown by officers and men of the leftist *Movimento das Forças Armadas* (Armed Forces Movement) on April 25, 1974. After fighting three major African colonial insurgencies for more than a decade and suffering almost 10,000 dead and another 30,000 wounded, the Portuguese military had reached its breaking point. As General Costa Gomes would later say bluntly, the country's armed forces had "reached the limits of neuro-psychological exhaustion."[2] Within the course of the next year, Angola, Cape Verde and Guinea-Bissau, and Mozambique would all emerge as newly independent states aligned with, if not beholden to, the Soviet Union. Moreover, this watershed would energize other African nationalist movements in the region—the African National Congress (ANC), the South West African People's Organization (SWAPO), the Zimbabwe African National Union (ZANU), and the Zimbabwe African People's Union (ZAPU)—to escalate their own armed struggles and in so doing usher in a prolonged period of chaos that would engulf southern Africa well beyond the end of the Cold War.

Taking center stage would be escalating conflicts in the newly independent and Marxist-led governments in Angola and Mozambique and the emergent bush wars in

The Portuguese leftist Armed Forces Movement stages a populist coup in Lisbon on April 25, 1974 that overthrows the government of Marcelo Caetano.

Rhodesia and South African-controlled South West Africa. These conflicts would span the entire spectrum of warfare—from ambushes by roving bands of guerillas armed with small arms to pitched battles involving thousands of conventional troops and the most modern weaponry. More than 20,000 heavily armed Cuban troops would come to the aid of Angolan government forces and clash headlong with South African mechanized forces on the savannahs and woodlands in the southern reaches of the country. Moscow would ship and airlift hundreds of millions of dollars in military equipment to its Angolan and Mozambican allies to stave off South African military aggression and counter rising domestic insurgencies. Likewise, hundreds of Soviet military personnel and technical advisers, along with East German and Cuban intelligence officers would be sent to southern Africa to assist their socialist brethren.

At the same time, the white minority governments in South Africa and Rhodesia would find themselves squarely in the crosshairs of this new onslaught. Guerrillas from the ANC, SWAPO, and ZANU / ZAPU were now able to operate directly into their territories from sanctuaries in neighboring Zambia, Angola and Mozambique. Rather than circle the wagons in a defensive laager, both Pretoria and Salisbury would embark on a no-holds-barred offensive strategy against their opponents. It would be a carrot-and-stick approach. If they could not persuade the leaders of Zambia, Angola and Mozambique—along with Tanzania the so-called Front Line States—to seek political accommodation and abandon support for their enemies, then Pretoria and Salisbury would be forced to unleash their full might against their neighbors. There would be no half measures. It was now very much a question of survival.

Over time the forces of confrontation would gain the upper hand, plunging southern Africa into a protracted period of instability and violence as all sides hardened their positions. Stepped up nationalist guerrilla attacks into Rhodesian and South African territory would be met by increasingly aggressive cross-border retaliatory raids. Punitive South African economic and trade policies against its neighbors would be countered by their creation of alternative economic and political structures, such as the Southern

Angola's first president, Agostinho Neto, quickly developed a close personal bond with Cuba's Fidel Castro.

Cuban combat troops would play a critical role in ensuring the survival of the MPLA government in the immediate aftermath of Angolan independence in 1975.

Africa Development Coordination Conference or SADCC. Growing anti-government domestic insurgencies in Angola and Mozambique would be relentlessly exploited by outside forces to destabilize these governments through the use of pro-Western proxy armies. At the same time both Luanda and Maputo would be increasingly driven into the welcoming arms of Moscow—and increasingly, in Mozambique's case, Beijing—and thus reinforcing the East–West divide.

The Soviet Union provided not only political and ideological support to the new Marxist government in Angola, but also the latest military equipment.

The election of Ronald Reagan to the U.S. presidency in 1980 and his hardline approach to countering the Soviet Union would further exasperate the East–West conflict with the implementation of the Reagan Doctrine. From Afghanistan to Angola and from Latin America to Southeast Asia, the centerpiece of American foreign policy would now be to aggressively confront and reverse Soviet expansionism and influence in the Third World through any means necessary. Washington would rely on the complete spectrum of power—diplomatic, economic, and military—to achieve its objectives and in doing so force Moscow to expend more and more resources to defend its global interests. For southern Africa this meant increasing covert military and financial assistance to Jonas Savimbi's UNITA in its fight against the Soviet-supported government of Aghostino Neto, and flirting with self-styled anti-communist movements throughout the region; or using the promise of U.S. economic and developmental assistance to woo governments away from anti-Western stances or finding political accommodation with apartheid South Africa to advance "constructive engagement" in the region. For the next two decades southern Africa's conflicts would play out along three distinct, yet deeply interwoven levels: at the national level as competing interests and ideologies battled for control over their country's future, at the regional level as Rhodesia and South Africa sought to destabilize hostile states or groups on its borders to ensure their own survival, and at the international level as the superpowers fueled an ever escalating level of violence in their quest to deny the other victory. This complex environment would repeatedly complicate peace efforts and, moreover, hamstring the ability of all participants to control the situation. Ultimately, it would take the collapse of the Soviet Union in 1991 and the death spiral of apartheid to finally open the door to achieving peace and reconciliation and even then the process would be a long and difficult one. For Mozambique this would come at a terrible price—sixteen years of unrelenting warfare and suffering, up to one million Mozambicans dead, millions more refugees in neighboring countries or made homeless, and a country lying in in ruins.

Regular Soviet ship visits to Luanda only served to reinforce Western and South African fears of Moscow's growing influence in the region.

2. THE ENEMY OF MY ENEMY

The sudden and unexpected collapse of Portuguese East Africa—Mozambique—presented a major strategic dilemma for the defense of the embattled white minority regimes in Rhodesia and South Africa. Not only had the rise of the newly independent and Marxist government in Mozambique in June 1975 exposed the entire 800-mile-long eastern frontier of Rhodesia to cross-border attacks, but it provided a new safe haven and operating base for the Zimbabwe African National Liberation Army (ZANLA), the military wing of Robert Mugabe's ZANU party. Likewise, South Africa was facing for the first time a hostile state directly on its border, a state whose leaders were politically aligned and supportive of groups, such as the ANC, that were committed to the armed struggle against apartheid. For the leadership in Salisbury and Pretoria this changed strategic environment would require a drastic reordering of the rules of the game if they were to survive. And thanks to a number of ill-conceived policies decisions early on, Mozambican President Samora Machel and his Frelimo party played directly into the hands of the Rhodesians and South Africans who had only to stoke the fire.

A Rising Threat from Mozambique

The aftermath of Mozambican independence drastically altered the Rhodesian and South African security calculus as efforts to reach a political accommodation or apply economic pressure failed to persuade President Machel to abandon his support for southern African liberation groups. With relations quickly deteriorating, both Salisbury and Pretoria opted to pursue military solutions, plunging Mozambique and its two immediate neighbors into a de facto state of war by early 1976. There would be no turning back now.

While a state of emergency had been ongoing in Rhodesia since the mid-1960s in response to rising African nationalism, the early 1970s saw an intensification of the bush war in the northeastern part of the country neighboring Mozambique, thanks in part to the growing ZANLA–Frelimo military alliance. Mozambican independence in 1975 only served to further fuel that relationship. By early 1976 Frelimo was facilitating the shipment of Chinese and East European arms to Zimbabwean guerrillas in Mozambique and allowing the establishment of ZANLA training camps and logistics bases in Manica and Tete provinces, directly opposite the Rhodesian border. Soon sources were reporting that an estimated 5,000–8,000 Zimbabwean guerrillas were residing inside Mozambique and preparing to infiltrate into Rhodesia.[1] This situation forced Salisbury to create new operational areas to counter rising infiltration along the Mozambican frontier: Operation Thrasher created in February 1976 along the eastern highlands and Operation Repulse in May 1976 in the southeast of the country.

Likewise, in an effort to disrupt ZANLA activity the Rhodesian military began sending small teams of elite operators from the Special Air Service (SAS) and the Selous Scouts

Independence comes to Mozambique on June 25, 1975.

Mozambique's first president, Samora Machel, was a veteran guerrilla fighter and a hardline Marxist, who was determined to transform the newly independent country.

Fidel Castro was an ardent supporter of both the Angolan and Mozambican revolutions.

on small-scale raids, ambushes, and sabotage operations, as well as on clandestine reconnaissance and intelligence-gathering missions. These activities, however, proved to be woefully inadequate in stemming cross-border infiltration. Thus, in August 1976 the Rhodesians launched their first full-scale, cross-border attack on ZANLA's Nyadzonya base camp along the Pungwe River, some 50 miles northeast of Umtali (now Mutare). The heavily armed flying column of Selous Scouts destroyed large quantities of supplies and inflicted more than 1,300 casualties.[2] While the Smith government considered the operation an overwhelming military success, ZANU claimed that many of those "massacred" were innocent refugees, stoking international and United Nations condemnation against Salisbury for the raid.[3] While direct confrontation with Frelimo forces was generally avoided during Rhodesian cross-border operations, some clashes were inevitable given the ZANLA pattern of co-locating is camps near Frelimo bases, which added to the rising tensions between the two countries.

To counter this increasing Rhodesian aggression, Mozambique turned to the Eastern Bloc for help, signing a Treaty of Friendship and Cooperation with the Soviet Union that included Moscow's pledge to assist Maputo in the event of a military attack. With the help of several hundred newly arriving Soviet and East European advisers, Mozambique also began to speed up the process of transforming the *Forças Popular de Libertação de Moçambique* (Popular Forces for the Liberation of Mozambique or FPLM) into a modern conventional military. Between 1977 and the end of 1978, the Soviet Union delivered hundreds of millions of dollars of military hardware, including 56 armored personnel carriers, 40 tanks (obsolete T-34/85s), antiaircraft missiles (including high altitude SA-3s), 43 MiG-21 fighters, and numerous pieces of heavy artillery and anti-tank missiles.[4]

Soviet military advisers first began arriving in Mozambique shortly after independence and would rise to some 800–1,000 by the late 1970s.

Above left: Rhodesian Prime Minister Ian Smith.

Above right: Lieutenant-General Peter Walls, commander of Rhodesian security forces.

This changing threat environment, as well as the deteriorating security situation inside Rhodesia meant that Prime Minister Ian Smith's forces were being increasingly stretched thin. Not only did this limit Rhodesian conventional military options in Mozambique, but it made them more risky and potentially costly. Something different needed to be done—and fast.

The Birth of an Insurgency

This was the situation that greeted Ken Flower, chief spymaster and head of the Rhodesian Central Intelligence Organization (CIO), in early 1977 as he and Rhodesian military commanders searched for a revamped strategy to counter the mounting threat from Mozambique. It needed to address not only the direct military threat posed by ZANLA infiltration, but one that also undermined Frelimo's ability and willingness to support Mugabe's forces in Mozambique. Moreover, it needed to be low-profile, operate on a shoestring budget, and not divert scarce military resources away from the war effort inside the Rhodesia. Such would be a tall order.

The Machel government was also facing its own problems. Beyond pressing foreign policy and security challenges, Frelimo was facing the monumental difficulty of uniting a highly diverse country, reforming a post-colonial economy, and building the new social-ist society that it envisioned. The party and its leadership would make many mistakes along the way by pushing too hard and alienating large elements of society, including traditional leaders and insti-tutions, like the Catholic Church; this created fertile ground for the coming insurgency. That Frelimo's ambitious efforts to recast Mozambique into a socialist state were met with political and social backlash was not entirely unexpected, but the degree of domes-tic opposition it fueled caught the new government off guard. Moreover, the willingness of Mozambican opposition elements to actively work with pariah minority regimes in Rhodesia and later South Africa would cause Frelimo to fatally underestimate the nature of the threat posed by the *bandidos armados* or armed bandits (as the government labeled them) to its survival.

Ken Flower, long-time head of the Rhodesian Central Intelligence Organization that would be instrumental in the creation and growth of Renamo.

While Rhodesian security officials had toyed for several years with the idea of developing a counterweight to

From very humble beginnings the Renamo insurgency would grow to become a serious challenge to the Frelimo government by the mid-1980s.

Frelimo by nurturing the domestic seeds of discontent, all their past attempts had failed. Efforts to recruit and co-opt pre-independence Frelimo splinter parties, like the *Comité Revolucionário de Moçambique* (COREMO), or political personalities such as Domingos Arouca all came to naught amid internal squabbling, personal ambitions, and competing agendas. Moreover, by 1977 none of the parties or leaders had much of a following or structure to mount any semblance of a resistance to Frelimo. Likewise, past efforts to make use of exiled white Portuguese settlers, former African colonial soldiers or members of disbanded Portuguese elite army units to mount sporadic attacks inside the country were either stillborn or ended in disaster.[5]

Surprisingly what was working was the Rhodesian CIO's psychological effort to sow the seeds of discord by those unhappy with many of Frelimo's new socialist policies. The center of this effort was *Voz da Africa Livre* (Voice of Free Africa), a radio station that began broadcasting in July 1976, utilizing a powerful transmitter that could be picked up throughout Mozambique. *Voz da Africa Livre* was manned by a handful of Mozambican exiles under the tutelage of Orlando Cristina, a 49-year-old white Mozambican from Niassa Province, and soon the station had gained a following among many disgruntled and anti-Frelimo Mozambicans. It also struck a nerve with the Machel regime, which called it "the voice of the hyena."[6] Most important by 1977 the station perpetuated the existence of a ghost military organization—the *Resistência Nacional Moçambicana* or

André Matsangaissa, Renamo's first military commander, was killed in battle in October 1979. (Photo André Thomashausen)

Renamo—in the minds of many Mozambicans seeking an alternative to Frelimo. It would now be up to the CIO to turn this mirage into a reality.

The catalyst for what was to become a real-life armed insurgency arrived in the form of a 26-year-old ex-Frelimo soldier, André Matsangaissa, who crossed the border into Rhodesia in October 1976. Initially disappointed by the lack of any concrete anti-Frelimo organization, Matsangaissa told Cristina that the only effective way to change the political situation in Mozambique "was by force of arms" and "that is what I intend to do."[7] When challenged by the CIO to return to Mozambique to raise an army of recruits, Matsangaissa did just that by successfully raiding the Sacuze re-education camp and freeing more than 50 prisoners on May 6, 1977.[8] About half these men opted to join Commander André, as he was now known, in forming the nucleus of the future insurgency and what Renamo would later label the Second War of Liberation. Ken Flower and the CIO had at last found their charismatic and audacious leader to implement their strategy.

The CIO based its Renamo operations out of an old abandon tobacco farm at Odzi, just west of the border town of Umtali. The base, which was established in late 1976, consisted of the main house that was used as the headquarters, stores building and instructors' housing, while the old tobacco barns were used to billet and feed the Renamo soldiers,

The Legend of Commander André

André Matade Matsangaissa joined Frelimo in 1972 and rose to platoon commander while operating in the Gorongosa area of central Mozambique that he called home. After independence he was assigned to the Engineering Corps near Beira, where he ran afoul of the government's anti-corruption purges in 1975 for allegedly stealing a Mercedes Benz for his personal use. He was convicted by a military tribunal and sent to the Sacuze re-education camp. The camp, located north of the Pungwe River and some 15 miles west of the town of Gorongosa (formerly Vila Paia de Andrada), was one of dozens of camps established by Frelimo in the center and north of the country to intern political opponents and disaffected Frelimo members. Matsangaissa's brother, however, maintains that the imprisonment was actually the result of André's vocal opposition to Frelimo policies and specifically to the government's confiscation of some of his family's property. Matsangaissa would eventually escape from Sacuze in October 1976 and made his way to Rhodesia where he sought out the *Voz da Africa Livre*'s Orlando Cristina.

When challenged by the Rhodesians to raise an army of recruits, Matsangaissa did just that by raiding government re-education camps to free prisoners, recruiting disgruntled former Frelimo guerrillas, and appealing to those with strong grievances against the government. Through his efforts Renamo grew into a military force of nearly 1,000 men by the end of 1978, operating across much of central Mozambique. A true Mozambican nationalist and ardent anti-Marxist, Matsangsissa chaffed at Rhodesian control over Renamo operations, but recognized it as a necessary evil in pursuit of his longer-term political objective of a popular uprising against Frelimo. Attuned to the psychological nature of guerrilla warfare, Matsangaissa also sought to gain the trust of the *povo* (the masses) and win them over to his cause through a "hearts and minds" strategy once Renamo established permanent bases inside Mozambique. André took great pains not to have his men become a burden on the already impoverished peasantry by distributing food, seeds, farming implements, and other looted supplies from government stores whenever possible and by making Renamo bases self-sufficient.

Early on Commander André, as he came to be known, developed a reputation for bravery and daring. Personally leading patrols deep into Mozambican territory, he and his men would operate on their own for up to 60 days conducting sabotage, intelligence-gathering, and launching attacks on enemy positions. Tactics were pretty simple and it was said that Matsangaissa would often initiate ambushes by leaping to his feet, fully exposing himself with gun above head at the start of the attack. In short order the *matsangos*, as locals nicknamed them after their leader, would come to be feared by both ZANLA and Frelimo forces for their ferocity in combat. Not surprisingly, Matsangaissa would meet his end on the battlefield while leading a counterattack against Frelimo forces near the town of Gorongosa in October 1979 at the age of 29. Nonetheless, his legacy as a Renamo's first commander and a revered guerrilla leader would endure with the post-war Renamo mayor of Beira erecting a statue and naming a square after him in 2008.

according to a former Rhodesian instructor.[9] The camp was encircled by a 20-foot-high earth embankment and security fence. Although officially a "secret base," it was commonly known by locals and the police as "the funny farm," because of the secrecy surrounding the activities going on there. Initially all the Renamo training officers at Odzi were Portuguese-speaking instructors, including some who undoubtedly had fought with the Portuguese army in Mozambique, but because of opposition by Matsangaissa they were quickly replaced with CIO instructors. This small team of four to five CIO officers—most were former SAS operators—was headed by Major Dudley Coventry, who was himself a former commander of the SAS.[10]

The growing Matsangaissa mystique and Cristina's broadcasts served as a rallying point for anti-Frelimo sentiment and proved instrumental in the recruitment in July 1977 of a young Frelimo officer from Sofala Province: Afonso Dhlakama. Dhlakama, the son of a

An abandoned tobacco farm at Odzi in eastern Rhodesia served as Renamo's rear base and CIO training and support facility until Zimbabwean independence. (Photo Danny Hartman)

Thanks to Rhodesian largesse, the ranks of Renamo guerrillas swelled from a few dozen in 1977 to nearly 3,000 well-trained men by early 1980. (Photo: Danny Hartman)

Shona-speaking Ndau traditional leader, was born in the southern part of Sofala Province in 1953. He was educated by Catholic seminarians in Beira and later conscripted into the Portuguese colonial army, but deserted in 1972 to join Frelimo. During the independence struggle he served as a Frelimo commander in the Niassa Province and after independence served as a logistics officer in Beira prior to his defection to Rhodesia. As Dhlakama rose to prominence within Renamo, the Frelimo government claimed he had been cashiered from the army for corruption and misconduct, thus his fleeing to Rhodesia. Dhlakama has personally disputed these charges, claiming that "he felt discriminated against on ethnic grounds, and that he had even obtained the necessary travel documents" and he "could not have done this if he were guilty of misconduct."[11]

Commander André apparently took an immediate liking to the short, bespectacled and bookish 24-year-old and within six months Dhlakama would become André's second-in-command. Much has been made by some observers of Dhlakama's rapid rise and the related downfall and disappearance of Matsangaissa's previous deputy, Orlando Macomo.[12] While there is certainly a dark side to Renamo and its internal power struggles, the downfall of Macomo can more simply be traced to a failed mine-laying operation in August 1977 and his subsequent attempt to cover it up. Once the truth came out, Macomo was transferred to Salisbury by the CIO and never heard from again.[13] Meanwhile, after having proven himself in the field and gained Matsangaissa's confidence, Dhlakama would be named Renamo's new deputy commander by the end of 1977.

A young Afonso Dhlakama, then Renamo's deputy commander, talking with CIO officer Danny Hartman in 1979 at Odzi. (Photo Danny Hartman)

With the Renamo leadership coming together, Ken Flower's goal of creating a small, highly capable guerrilla force was finally becoming a reality. The new organization would act as "the eyes and ears" of Rhodesian intelligence, with a primary focus on gathering information about ZANLA bases and its movements inside Mozambique.[14] On a limited scale Renamo forces would also have the capability to strike at Mozambican economic and political targets to increase the cost to Frelimo of supporting ZANLA forces.[15] Thus, the new guerrilla force was being groomed by the CIO to play a very limited and tightly controlled part of the Rhodesian war strategy: there was no question as to who was in charge and calling shots. By September 1977 Renamo was able to put 76 fighters in the field, rising to 288 at the beginning of 1978, and ultimately reaching 914 by the end of the year.[16]

Battlefield Central Mozambique

As the bush war inside Rhodesia heated up, the Smith government began taking increasingly risky measures to stem the flow of Zimbabwean guerrillas infiltrating into the country. Once given the green light, the Rhodesian security forces unleashed a wave of cross-border raids—or "externals" as they were called—against suspected guerrillas bases, infiltration routes, and supply lines in Mozambique in the hope of disrupting ZANLA operations and buying time for a favorable political settlement. Over the next several years, Smith's forces would mount some two dozen major operations and other smaller raids and air attacks against Zimbabwean and Frelimo forces and installations in Mozambique.[17]

The worsening Rhodesian security situation and the continuing ZANLA buildup in Mozambique drove Salisbury to significantly escalate its attacks beginning in 1977. Not only would these operations become more numerous and widespread along the frontier, but they would strike increasingly deeper into Mozambican territory. In November 1977 the Rhodesians launched Operation Dingo, the largest and most ambitions attack on ZANLA infrastructure so far. Over the course of several days, some 200 airborne SAS and Rhodesian Light Infantry (RLI) troops supported by Canberra

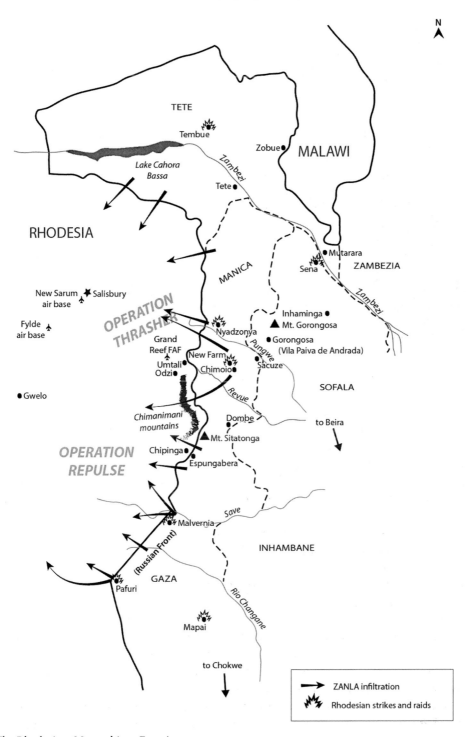

The Rhodesian–Mozambican Frontier, 1977–1979.

Following Mozambican independence, Frelimo sought to transform its guerrilla forces into a conventional army with Soviet and Eastern Bloc assistance to counter the Rhodesian and South African military threats. (Photo Centro de Formação Fotografica, Maputo, Mozambique)

bombers and Hunter fighter-bombers assaulted ZANLA's main headquarters complex at Chimoio some 75 miles from the Rhodesian border, as well as the Tembué camp located northeast of the Cahora Bassa Dam. The attack on Chimoio, which was estimated to house 9,000–11,000 guerrillas, recruits, and support staff, as well as tons of supplies, was deemed an overwhelming success. It produced the "biggest kill rate of any camp attack of the war;" more than 2,000 were killed and thousands more believed wounded.[18] It also once again provoked international condemnation, but the Rhodesian generals felt they had little choice but to take the war to ZANLA in Mozambique and things were about to get a lot worse for Mugabe and his Frelimo hosts.

While Renamo guerrillas often worked directly with Rhodesian security forces to provide intelligence and real-time reconnaissance support for externals, they were also now tasked by Flower to "perpetuate or create instability in areas of Mozambique."[19] Renamo forces, now operating in larger groups of 30 to 60 men, increasingly began to target central Mozambique's economic infrastructure and lines of communication. Bridges and telephone lines were sabotaged, dams and power plants rocketed. Roads were mined or subject to ambush and trains were shot up or derailed. While most early operations were conducted close to the Rhodesian frontier in the Catandica and Pungwe River basin areas and north of the Chimanimani salient in Manica Province, Renamo fighters began ranging well into Sofala Province by 1978. Here the Beira—Chimoio road

Machel's granting of safe haven to ZANLA guerrillas following Mozambican independence brought the wrath of the Rhodesian military down on his country from 1976 to 1979.

By the late 1970s, Rhodesia was fighting for its survival in the face of an ever escalating insurgency.

A Rhodesian fire force loads up for action on Alouette IIIs.

and rail line, the Dondo–Inhaminga rail corridor, and the road south of Inchope fell under near constant attack. Effectively using hit-and-run tactics, Renamo units sowed havoc across the region, forcing Frelimo to divert forces to safeguard ZANLA supply lines and protect vital economic infrastructure. Although often willing to take on isolated FPLM positions or ZANLA guerrillas if the opportunity presented itself, Renamo commanders for the most part avoided going head to head with their more heavily armed adversaries, preferring to live and fight another day.

The combination of cross-border externals and Renamo harassing attacks were certainly taking their toll by the end of 1978, leaving a trail of death and destruction in their wake and inflicting hundreds of millions of dollars to the Mozambican economy. Yet even then they failed to stem the tide of ZANLA infiltration into Rhodesia or persuade President Machel to abandon his support for Mugabe. As Machel apparently saw it, the best way to bring an end to the Rhodesian and South African threat to his country was to bring about the liberation of Zimbabwe (and eventually South Africa) by remaining steadfast in his support for Mugabe while at the same time increasing the potential cost of armed aggression by strengthening his own military forces.

Renamo's new mandate from the CIO and its growing appeal in disaffected regions of the country, however, effectively energized the insurgency going into 1979 and raised the specter of a formidable challenge to Frelimo's grip on power. Nonetheless, Frelimo's leadership found it difficult to take Renamo seriously, preferring instead to see the guerrillas as nothing more than *bandidos armados*. They were nothing more than common thieves and criminals acting as surrogates for white racist regimes in Salisbury and Pretoria and thus could be easily dismissed. It would prove to be a serious miscalculation by Frelimo.

The 1950s-era Hawker Hunters played an important role as strike aircraft during Rhodesian military operations in Mozambique.

An attempted Frelimo counterattack against Rhodesian forces attacking ZANLA's New Chimoio base during Operation Miracle in late 1979 ended in disaster with the loss of several APCs to Rhodesian strikes.

3. MISSED OPPORTUNITIES

In retrospect the two-year period from 1979 to 1980 would be a defining point in the Mozambican war, notable for the missed opportunities by both Frelimo and Renamo to decisively change the course of the conflict and likely bring the war to an end. Instead, the tide of battle would fail to change for either side, resulting in a protracted struggle that doomed the country and its people to 12 more years of a grinding war, widespread destruction, and the deaths of up to one million Mozambicans. There would be wild swings of euphoria and optimism by both Frelimo and Renamo, only to have their hopes dashed by the harsh reality of pursuing victory on the battlefield. For like most civil war situations, peace is usually achieved at the negotiating table rather than on the field of battle, a cruel lesson that both would have to learn the hard way.

The Pressure Builds on Frelimo

Up until now the more capable Rhodesian security forces had carried the burden of destabilizing Mozambique through external operations in the course of their battle with ZANLA and collateral attacks against FPLM. Renamo was growing and becoming more effective,

The challenging drop zone high atop Mt. Gorongosa. (Photo John Reid-Rowland)

Rhodesian Air Force C-47 "Dakota" transport aircraft conducting Operation Bumper resupply flight in October 1979. (Photo John Reid-Rowland)

but Matsangaissa still had less than 1,000 men under his command in January 1979 and their operational reach was constrained by the need to operate out of eastern Rhodesia. This would all change by the final half of the year. Renamo would establish permanent bases deep inside Mozambique and widen the number and scope of operations. A more than doubling in the size of the guerrilla force would set the insurgents on the path toward self-sufficiency, even as South Africa made its initial foray into the conflict.

Up to this time Renamo guerrillas had been largely operating on their own inside Mozambique, albeit with extensive Rhodesian logistical support and operational guidance from the CIO. However, with Smith's need to increase the pressure on ZANLA and President Machel now that an estimated 13,000 nationalist guerrillas were operating inside Rhodesia,[1] a more aggressive strategy was required, one with a much greater role for Renamo. According to the 1979 *Short-Term Strategy for Mozambique* this entailed a number of specific tasks including obtaining maximum support from South Africa, fostering greater instability in Mozambique, supporting anti-communist and anti-Frelimo groups, and minimizing Frelimo's support to ZANLA and its opposition to the newly elected Zimbabwe-Rhodesia government of national unity.[2] For the Rhodesian security forces this meant additional emphasis on externals and special operations in Mozambique, as well as greater "liaison and guidance," "the provision of ... logistic support, and strategic and tactical advice," as well as "greater coordination of effort" with Renamo to improve the insurgents' effectiveness.[3] Renamo apparently was increasingly becoming a key part of the solution to addressing the Mozambican problem.

Although still under CIO control, the SAS would now become the primary operational conduit for supporting Matsangaissa's forces in the field. In addition to serving as operational planners, advisers, and specialized trainers (in explosives and demolition for example), small SAS call signs of three to four men would now be regularly accompanying Renamo fighters—armed with AK-47s, RPG-7s, 60-mm and 82-mm mortars, and anti-vehicle mines—on deep-penetration missions into Mozambique. Once Renamo had established permanent bases inside Mozambique after August 1979, larger-size SAS call signs would then be routinely deployed to these bases for periods of up to six weeks. Given the huge demand late in the Rhodesian war for SAS operators (not only in Mozambique, but also in Zambia and Botswana) there were never enough personnel to go around and the SAS commander, Lieutenant-Colonel Garth Barrett, was never able to deploy more than two dozen men with Renamo at any one time.[4] Nonetheless, the SAS presence was felt well out of proportion to its numbers, because not only did the teams provide expertise and boost the morale and confidence among the young guerrilla fighters, but they also gave Renamo units direct radio communications with Odzi for the first time. Prior to this, messages were hand-carried, which often negated their timeliness and intelligence value.

This new partnership proved immediately fruitful. In January a joint force attacked and destroyed the Mavuze hydroelectric power station at the Chicamba Real Dam about 25 miles east of Umtali. This was followed by the high-profile sabotage of Beira's fuel storage depot in late March by a SAS–South African commando team, but publicly claimed by Renamo.

ZANLA's lines of communication and its logistics network were constantly under attack by both Renamo and SAS teams throughout the first half of the year with the Tete–Mutarara rail line north of the Zambezi River being sabotaged for the first time

in April. Farther afield, Renamo troops were steadily advancing far southwest of Manica Province, attacking and seizing the town of Machaze, just north of the Save River in July. Meanwhile, other joint units were busy attacking vehicular traffic along the road south of Inchope, including one ambush that appeared to kill three East German advisers.[5] Critically, these SAS-teamed units could now call on Rhodesian air support for extraction or air strikes to ward off pursuing enemy forces.

It was, however, the establishment of permanent Renamo bases inside Mozambican territory, greater direct South African assistance, and the unleashing of the military to leverage Salisbury's negotiating position in peace talks that allowed the Rhodesians to exponentially ratchet up the pressure on ZANLA and Frelimo forces in the final quarter of the year.

Regarded as a brave and charismatic leader, "Commander André" instilled great loyalty among Renamo cadres by personally leading his troops in combat. (Photo Danny Hartman)

First, in late August the long anticipated process of establishing permanent Renamo bases inside Mozambique, which would permit the guerrillas to conduct larger and more sustained operations, got underway with Matsangaissa leading a 300-man Renamo battalion into the Gorongosa region from Odzi. By September 5, André had set up a central camp that would serve as Renamo's new headquarters and recruiting base on the Gorongosa mountaintop. Buoyed by an influx of new local recruits, Matsangaissa was able to expand Renamo's operational presence all the way from the Pungwe–Vanduzi river basin north of the main Umtali–Chimoio road eastward through the Gorongosa region to Inhaminga and up northwesterly to the Marringue–Macossa area. Likewise, another 300-man battalion moved from Odzi in early October to establish a new Renamo base in Manica Province just west of the Chimanimani Mountains near Gogoi. From there the guerrillas began operating between the Revué and the Buzi rivers, as well as across into western Sofala Province toward Muxunge and National Highway 1.

Second, thanks to the rise of Defence Minister P. W. Botha to prime minister in late 1978, the South Africans adopted a more supportive and reinvigorated stance toward the Rhodesian war effort. Thus, by early 1979 Pretoria's troops returned to the fight, South African helicopters and bombers were actively participating in combat operations, joint training was underway again, and military supplies and equipment were once again helping to fuel the Rhodesian war machine. At the time of the December 1979 ceasefire Pretoria may have had more than 5,000 personnel and more than a dozen aircraft fighting alongside Rhodesian forces.

Operation Bumper

Once Renamo established its own bases inside Mozambique, starting with the Gorongosa camp in September 1979, the Rhodesian military assumed a larger and more direct role in supporting the insurgents. Known as Operation Bumper, which last from September to December 1979, both the Special Air Service (SAS) and the Rhodesian Air Force provided critical support that allowed Renamo to move toward the path of self-sufficiency inside Mozambique. Using three- to four-man SAS call signs that were rotated in and out of the country by air on a six-week basis, the SAS helped the insurgents site their defenses, provided on-site training to new locally recruited men, served in an advisory role to the local Renamo commander, and passed time-sensitive intelligence reports back to Renamo's rear base at Odzi.

The air force air component of Operation Bumper consisted of aging, but amazingly reliable, Dakota C-47 transport aircraft from No. 3 Squadron as well as helicopters from No. 7 (Alouette III) and No. 8 (Agusta Bell-205) squadrons providing an air bridge between Rhodesia and Renamo bases inside Mozambique. The primary destination for most of these missions was the Gorongosa plateau, which rose conspicuously some

4,000 feet above the flat countryside and was located about 115 miles from Umtali (now Mutare). Other occasional supply drops were made to Renamo's southern base in the Gogoi area, which lies opposite the Chipinga border district of Rhodesia. Despite having men and equipment stretched to the breaking point in the latter half of 1979, the air force was able to mount an impressive logistics effort over the three-and-a-half-month life of the operation that delivered more than 55 tons of weapons, ammunition, food, and other supplies to Renamo forces in Mozambique.

Standard operating procedure required one to three Dakotas, or "Daks" as they were called, carrying up to 4,000 pounds of cargo, flying the two-hour-40-minute round trip from Salisbury's New Sarum airbase to Gorongosa every seven to 15 days and about once a month to the smaller southern base at Gogoi. Helicopters, mostly operating out of the forward airfield at Grand Reef near Umtali, were used mainly to uplift the departing SAS call signs, collect the used cargo parachutes, conduct the occasional emergency supply run or provide casualty evacuation. The drop zone at Gorongosa, known as Bumper North, was a small clearing high on the plateau that was covered with woods and streams that often challenged the skill and nerves of the Dak pilots. While the drop zone for Bumper South at Gogoi was not as majestic a venue as the Gorongosa plateau, it too required the complete attention of the pilots, because it was not as obvious and relied on the SAS man on the ground for directions and when to start the drop.

In addition to the often harsh flying conditions, Frelimo was becoming increasingly adept at setting up air ambushes. The Gorongosa drop zone was especially dangerous given its limited approach options with enemy small-arms fire a frequent threat to the planes approaching at 500 feet. "I was the lead Dak," recalls one former Bumper pilot, "and thank goodness the ground gunners hadn't been trained in lead shooting—all the ack-ack round passed behind me. Not a round hit ... but [the dispatcher in the back] was scared witless by the racket of the rounds cracking by the door." Although the Dakotas were only occasionally fired on, the lower and slower-flying helicopters were particularly vulnerable to mobile antiaircraft columns using 37-mm and 12.7-mm weapons or "Frelimo mobiles," as they came to be known. Acting on reports of aircraft activity inbound into Mozambique, the Frelimo mobiles would try to position themselves along the expected return flight path in the hope of catching the aircraft returning to Rhodesia. At least one helicopter was shot down this way in October 1979.

The signing of the Lancaster House peace agreement on December 21, 1979 brought the Rhodesian war and Operation Bumper to a close, but not before one last push was made—with South African assistance—to provide Renamo forces in Mozambique with a golden handshake of nearly 40,000 pounds of supplies on December 16. Bumper was over, but the war inside Mozambique would go on.

Source: S. Emerson, *The Battle for Mozambique*, pp. 42-46.

The most immediate impact for Renamo of this new South African involvement was in the area of logistics support via Operation Bumper that came at a critical time with the Rhodesian Air Force's Dakota cargo transport fleets stretched to the limit. It therefore was with great relief that in early October South African Air Force (SAAF) C-130 transports began routinely flying Bumper resupply missions. With their larger payload the C-130s were able to able to airdrop large quantities of arms, ammunition, food and supplies to Renamo bases. A typical C-130 load, for example, would consist of 300 AK-47s, 98,000 rounds of 7.62-mm ammo, 75 82-mm and 100 60-mm mortar bombs, four RPG-7 launchers and 40 rockets, and 24 Claymore mines, plus several thousand kilograms of food and other supplies.[6] Operating out of the more remote Fylde airfield near Hartley (now Chegutu), the SAAF aircraft and crew normally arrived early afternoon for the loading of supplies and a preflight briefing. Although they would fly missions to both Renamo's northern Gorongosa and southern Gogoi bases, they were more commonly used for larger supply runs to the main headquarters at Gorongosa.

Although less impactful at the time, the appointment of Colonel Cornelius "Charlie" van Niekerk to serve as South Africa liaison to the CIO's Mozambique Desk and its Renamo operation would prove momentous for the future of the insurgency and its evolution in the years ahead. In the near term, van Niekerk worked to provide the CIO with 4,500 small arms, uniforms, and personal kit items from South African stocks to meet the growing needs of the insurgents.[7] To assist in the infiltration and exfiltration of guerrillas across the Mozambican border, Pretoria also provided some seven vehicles, including heavy-duty trucks, to the Odzi base. South African intelligence also provided some level of funding to the insurgents in 1979; although the amount is unknown, it was reportedly planned to commit over $1 million in 1980.[8]

Finally, with Rhodesian peace talks slated to begin in London in early September, Salisbury's military commanders sought to up the ante by striking as hard as ever at ZANLA's war infrastructure and unleashing their wrath on the fragile Mozambican economy as a way to gain concessions at the negotiating table. On September 5, Operation Uric was launched with the goal of disrupting rising ZANLA infiltration into southeast Rhodesia by destroying Frelimo's supporting logistics and communication infrastructure. Key bridges along the Malvernia–Barragem rail and road corridor were targeted and FPLM's 2 Brigade headquarters at Mapai that was coordinating operations was also slated for destruction. During the course of three days 360 Rhodesian soldiers, supported by Hunter and Lynx (Cessna 337) ground-attack aircraft and Canberra bombers, would be airlifted up to 200 miles deep into Gaza Province and engaged in minelaying, sabotaging bridges, and fighting pitch battles with entrenched FPLM soldiers.[9] The Rhodesian Air Force also conducted more than a dozen air strikes against FPLM troops and installations, dropping 500- and 1,000-pound bombs, as well as anti-personnel cluster munitions. While the operation was successfully in downing numerous bridges, interdicting roads, and heavily damaging economic infrastructure, the Rhodesians were unable to completely cut ZANLA's supply lines or capture Mapai. Moreover, it came at a high price—the loss of 18 men and two helicopters, one of which was South African.[10]

Meanwhile back in central Mozambique, roving Renamo guerrillas and SAS call signs were unleashing their own mini-offensive against lines of communication, by blowing bridges, mining and ambushing road and rail traffic, and attacking isolated FPLM garrisons. The important Frelimo communication relay facility high atop Mt. Xilvuo in western Sofala Province was heavily damaged on September 12 and this was followed about a week later by the sinking of two dredgers in Beira harbor by a team of South African and Rhodesian commandos.[11] And things were about to get a lot worse. On September 29 the Rhodesians launched Operation Miracle against ZANLA's main base at New Chimoio, located some 30 miles northeast of Umtali, using airmobile RLI troops and a heavily armed flying column led by Eland armored cars and supported by a half dozen World War II-vintage 25-pounder artillery pieces.

The sprawling 25-square-mile base complex was dominated by tall outcroppings (nicknamed "Monte Cassino" by the Rhodesians) and was heavily defended by a series of bunkers, trench complexes, and an array of antiaircraft weapons.[12] It was thought to contain about 2,000 guerrilla fighters and recruits, as well as large quantities of weapons and supplies. The initial air strikes went off without a hitch, but the flying column became bogged down and encountered stiffer resistance from what turned out to be an enemy force three times larger than anticipated. The strong resistance, especially from atop the heavily defended Monte Cassino, allowed ZANLA forces to make a fairly

An SAS call sign prepares to deploy into central Mozambique, late 1979. (Photo courtesy Craig Fourie)

orderly withdrawal by day three of the battle. Large quantities of equipment and supplies were either captured or destroyed during the mop-up operations, but ZANLA appeared to suffer only several hundred dead. Rhodesian casualties were few, but the Rhodesian Air Force lost three value aircraft, including a Canberra bomber lost during a bombing run against Monte Cassino and a Hunter strike aircraft shot down while fending off an armored FPLM counterattack on October 3.[13]

Just as the operational tempo was building, disaster struck for Renamo when its charismatic leader, André Matsangaissa, was killed in battle on October 17. As André's deputy, Afonso Dhlakama took over command despite some internal grumbling and was soon directing operations from the movement's Gorongosa base. It would take some time before Dhlakama was able to consolidate complete control over the insurgency and undercurrents of discontent would ripple through the ranks for some time until they were finally resolved in late 1980.

The last few months of 1979 would see some of the most intense fighting so far across the entire region as the Rhodesian war neared its climax. While the politicians at the Lancaster House peace talks argued over the terms of a settlement in London, their respective militaries attempted to deliver the coup de grâce to the enemy. ZANLA commanders sought to push as many guerrillas (now supplemented by FPLM regulars) as they could into the Rhodesian countryside, while rival nationalist leader Joshua Nkomo prepared his Zimbabwe People's Revolutionary Army (ZIPRA) for a conventional thrust across the Zambian frontier. At the same time the Rhodesian military was planning to cripple the Mozambican economy and finally force Machel to abandon his support to Mugabe. Given the priority of addressing the threat posed by Nkomo's Soviet-equipped battalions of armored cars and tanks, the Rhodesian security forces turned their focus to Zambia, launching three major operations in a 45-day period. Lacking the manpower and matériel to unleash the same level of destruction on Mozambique, Salisbury relied on the SAS and its Renamo partners to deliver the knockout blow and bring Frelimo to its knees.

Despite intense FPLM pressure on its Gorongosa stronghold following Matsangaissa's death, Renamo guerrillas remained on the offensive. Although Frelimo forces were able to root out the insurgents from a number of their positions in the Gorongosa region during this time, they were unable to destroy Dhlakama's forces or capture Renamo's central base. The underlying reason for this could be found in FPLM's changed makeup. While FPLM units—now fitted out with armored personnel carriers, heavy artillery, anti-aircraft missiles, and even tanks—were making life increasingly dangerous and costly for Rhodesian cross-border operations, these same units were also proving themselves incapable of hunting down Renamo guerrillas and their SAS partners. When faced with overwhelming enemy numbers, Renamo fighters and SAS call signs would simply melt away into the bush to live to fight another day or call in Rhodesian air strikes on the road-bound columns.

By early November, the SAS and the Rhodesian Air Force had successfully destroyed or severely damaged all major bridges over the Zambezi River in the Tete–Moatize area, as well as damaging the critical Sena railroad bridge downriver. Renamo forces

The venerable C-47 transports, known as "Daks," did yeoman duty for the Rhodesian Air Force by conducting airdrops of both men and supplies in Mozambique.

meanwhile attacked the important rail and road center at Inhaminga and cut road and telephone communications between Catandica and Vanduzi in northern Manica. In the southern operational zone, Lucas Mulhanga with a 300-man battalion established a new base on Sitatonga Mountain, at the southern end of the Chimanimani salient overlooking the Lucite River. By December, Renamo had deployed nearly two battalions (some 500–600 men) into the northern operational zone centered on Gorongosa and nearly another three additional battalions (about 800 men total) into the southern operational zone. Renamo was now active in about three-fourths of Manica and Sofala provinces. This period also saw the foreshadowing of a new kind of violence, with the Mozambican press reporting that in early December Renamo guerrillas carried out a vengeance raid on the Manica border town of Espungabera, killing and decapitating Frelimo officials and then impaling their heads on stakes.[14]

Even under this blistering military campaign, Machel remained defiant knowing the end of the Rhodesian conflict was fast approaching. Although tacitly acknowledging his army's inability to wipe out Renamo given its Rhodesian support, Frelimo did not opt to remain passively on the defense. Soviet and Eastern Bloc weapons continued to flow into the country as Machel sought to strengthen his military. Likewise, FPLM forces mounted numerous search and destroy operations across the central provinces to keep Renamo off-balance and maintain pressure on the insurgents' Mozambican bases. And despite the growing pressure on ZANLA, it continued to push men and arms across the border into Rhodesia.

Then it was over. On December 21, 1979 the warring parties to the Rhodesian conflict formally signed the Lancaster House peace agreement that ended the bloodshed and would bring about Zimbabwean independence. A ceasefire was to take hold on December 28 and elections were to be held in early 1980. Of more direct impact on the fighting inside Mozambique was the message from Rhodesian military headquarters calling that "all external calls signs are to be withdrawn from Mozambique, Botswana, and Zambia immediately."[15] Although not unexpected, the actual announcement probably came as a severe shock to SAS men on the ground in Mozambique, and even more so to Renamo fighters whose fate was now uncertain. They needn't have worried. For only one day later, another highly sensitive message from the Rhodesian high command would order the continuation of Operation Bumper.[16] The war in Mozambique would still go on.

The Dawning of a New Day
With Mugabe's ZANU party's unexpected election victory in early March 1980 and the approach of Zimbabwean independence on April 18, Renamo was set to lose not only its rear base, logistical support, and communications network, but its psychological patronage as well. To make matters even worse, a newly reenergized Frelimo was turning its attention to vanquishing the armed bandits inside Mozambique now that the Rhodesia military threat was gone. Alone and increasingly isolated, the insurgency was in deep trouble.

Dhlakama, however, needn't have worried. Unbeknown to him and his fighters, Flower and the CIO were making preparations to transfer the entire operation lock, stock, and barrel to South Africa.[17] The handover took place in three stages over the course of several days amid the post-election confusion. First, Orlando Cristina and the staff of *Voz da Africa Livre* along with the mobile transmitter at Gwelo were flown out to South Africa. Next, an SAS team drove seven Renamo vehicles loaded with equipment and arms from Odzi to South Africa. And finally 250 or so new trainees at Odzi along with Coventry and several other CIO officers were airlifted to Waterkloof airbase just outside Pretoria. Upon arrival, this group was sent to a hastily erected bush camp near Kruger National Park along the banks of the Letaba River. Differences between the former Rhodesian handlers and their new South African hosts over the management and future direction of Renamo, however, soon led to a break between the two sides. Coventry and all but one of his team returned to Zimbabwe, leaving the South Africans solely in charge. While Renamo had found a new patron, Matsangaissa's dream of fomenting a new Mozambican nationalist movement as an alternative to Frelimo would once again have to take a backseat to Pretoria's agenda as the price to be paid for the insurgency's survival.

Although Renamo's long-term prospects had certainly brightened, its situation inside Mozambique continued to deteriorate following Zimbabwean independence with the tide shifting in Frelimo's favor. Since the start of the year FPLM forces had finally overrun Renamo's Gorongosa Mountain base and continuing pressure and dwindling supplies forced Dhlakama to order a general withdrawal to south of the Beira–Umtali road at the end of April. To make matters worse Lucas Mhlanga, the southern operational base commander, appeared to be colluding to break away from Dhlakama and become the new conduit for South African aid to Renamo.[18]

Once Dhlakama arrived at Sitatonga with his depleted force of several hundred men, he moved to reassert his leadership and rally Renamo's demoralized forces. Simmering tensions within the ranks had been building for some time and recent setbacks apparently encouraged Mhlanga to exploit the situation to burnish his standing at Dhlakama's expense. The resulting showdown has since assumed mythical status, climaxing with the now legendary and widely repeated "shoot out" between Dhlakama and Mhlanga factions at Renamo's "Chisumbanje base in June 1980" that resulted in Mhlanga's death, according to multiple published histories of Renamo.[19] This story, however, is pure fiction. In reality Dhlakama had largely consolidated his position within Renamo by obtaining the over-whelming support of old-line Renamo field commanders and the guerrilla ranks in the eight months since Matsangaissa's death. Moreover, although Mhlanga was able to exercise a fair degree of operational independence in the southern zone and had strong

President Machel had hoped that the ending of the Rhodesian war with the Lancaster House agreement in December 1979 would spell the end of the Renamo insurgency, but it was not to be. (File photo)

Robert Mugabe and the senior ZANU leaders returning home to joyous crowds in December 1979; in a few short months he would become prime minister of a newly independent Zimbabwe. Rex Nhongo, his senior ZANLA general, is to Mugabe's right, facing.

personal relationships with some of his Rhodesian mentors, he was nonetheless a fairly junior commander, having only joined Renamo in early 1979. Any attempted power grab by him would have undoubtedly faced considerable opposition from older, more experienced field commanders.

Once confronted with Mhlanga's insubordination upon his arrival at Sitatonga in May 1980, Dhlakama had Mhlanga arrested and imprisoned.[20] To further underscore his position, Dhlakama was named President and Supreme Military Commander of Renamo in June.[21] Mhlanga was later released; he helped set up the new Renamo base at Chicarre in southern Manica Province and continued to serve as a field commander until the end of 1980 when he was again imprisoned, according to a former Renamo combatant.[22] Subsequently, he was transferred to South Africa, where he then disappeared from the scene.

In addition to sorting out Renamo's internal divisions, Dhlakama and his men were confronting a dramatically changed battlefield and serious operational challenges given their heavy losses in men and territory, as well as yet unproven South African supply line. A major South African air resupply of 19 tons of ammunition and supplies on June 20 augured well,[23] but Sitatonga's isolated location up high in the rugged mountainous region was fast becoming a strategic liability with the hostile Zimbabwean border to the

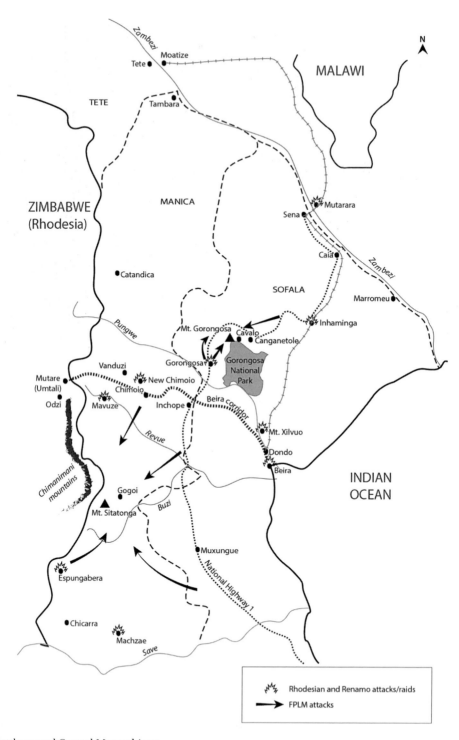

Battleground Central Mozambique.

Britain's long suffering "Rhodesian problem" comes to an end in April 1980 with the lowering of the Union Flag.

west and Frelimo forces on the move from the south and east. Moreover, Dhlakama could muster just 800–900 men at the base with 300–400 additional fighters scattered across smaller Renamo camps in southern Manica and Sofala provinces, just as Frelimo was preparing to deliver a knockout blow.

Operation Leopard was to be the final nail in Renamo's coffin. Even before Dhlakama had regrouped his forces and consolidated his position at Sitatonga, FPLM forces were already on the move. The plan involved deploying troops along the Save River border with Gaza Province to prevent Renamo guerrillas fleeing southward while elements of 2 Brigade sweeping northward from the Save river would drive toward the Buzi River. At the same time the main attack force drawn from 3 and 4 Brigades would move down from the Beira transportation corridor and push westward along the Buzi in the direction of the Zimbabwe, where Mugabe promised to seal the border. A third FPLM force was given permission to transit Zimbabwe and would launch its attack from the border town of Espungabera toward Sitatonga itself. The Mozambican air force would also be used to bomb suspected guerrilla concentrations and to provide air support when needed. If all worked as planned Renamo would be trapped by the three converging columns and completely destroyed.

The offensive got off to a good start, forcing the outnumbered and outgunned Renamo forces to fall back toward their base at Sitatonga. By late June, Frelimo forces had reached the foot of Sitatonga Mountain where the guerrillas stiffened their resistance by

Lord Christopher Soames, as the newly appointed Governor of Zimbabwe-Rhodesia, was given the unenviable task of ensuring the peace in the run-up to elections and Zimbabwean independence.

taking advantage of the rugged favorable terrain. In response, the attacking FPLM forces unleashed a prolonged artillery and air bombardment before launching their ground assault. It proved too much for the exhausted defenders, who were forced to abandon their positions and flee. Sitatonga fell to FPLM troops in the first days of July. Frelimo trumpeted this major success over the armed bandits with the capture of Renamo's main southern base, the killing of 272 guerrilla fighters, and the capturing of another 300 more.[24]

Still, despite this setback, Dhlakama and the majority of his men escaped and would live to continue the fight, albeit on a smaller scale, while they licked their wounds. Make no mistake about it, the 1980 Frelimo offensives against Gorongosa and Sitatonga had seriously crippled Renamo. The insurgents lost their key bases, were now short of weapons and supplies, combat strength had been cut by more than half, and they were now confined to a vastly restricted operational area. Renamo was on the ropes. An unintended consequence of this successful campaign, however, was Frelimo's mistaken belief that Renamo had all but been defeated. Or so Machel thought.

Toward An Uncertain Future

Although Renamo forces inside Mozambique were just barely hanging on in late 1980, the relocation of its rear base, *Voz da Africa Livre*, and supporting infrastructure to South Africa, as well as its budding relationship with South African military intelligence under the tutelage of Colonel van Niekerk gave Dhlakama hope for the future of the insurgency. A new training base was carved out of the virgin bush at Letaba Ranch on the outskirts of Kruger National Park in the Eastern Transvaal and staffed with South African recce commando instructors.[25] Renamo's administrative and communications headquarters was set up at Sawong, just south of Phalaborwa in the Eastern Transvaal, providing a direct link to Renamo commanders in the field.[26] Most important of all, the South African Air Force was airdropping supplies and equipment to Renamo's newly established main base at Chicarre (also known as Garagua), north of the Save River in southern Manica Province.

The move to South Africa also would result in some critical organizational restructuring that would have a dramatic impact on the evolution and legitimacy of the insurgency in the years to come. While Dhlakama was clearly the face of the resistance inside Mozambique and the cornerstone of the military effort, van Niekerk sought to develop and enhance the political image of the insurgency; one that Pretoria could control and manipulate. To that end Orlando Cristina assumed new importance as Renamo's secretary general in November 1980 and went about creating an overseas network of Renamo representatives in Europe and North America. He would play a leading role in the effort to recast Renamo as a broader and more robust political-military organization capable of overthrowing the Machel government. Although not the first choice of South African intelligence officials, who had flirted with other exiled Mozambican political leaders, Cristina was able to outmaneuver his opponents and gain reluctant acquiesce from Dhlakama to become the external face of the movement.[27] Lingering questions over Cristina's tainted colonial past, his association with white Mozambicans and the expatriate Portuguese community, and allegations over diversions of funds, however, would taint his leadership role. Moreover, it would awaken developing fissures between the guerrilla fighters inside Mozambique and their external political network that would last throughout the war. This last factor would end up having a very profound and negative impact on Renamo and complicate peace negotiations later on. But none of that mattered now as there was a war to fight.

Somewhat surprisingly both sides entered 1981 on an optimist note. Frelimo forces had taken advantage of the collapse of the Rhodesian lifeline and the advent of Zimbabwean independence to score major battlefield gains, including overrunning Renamo's two main bases and driving the remnants of Dhlakama's army into the hinterland. Low-level insurgent and bandit activity—it was often hard to tell one from the other—still continued in parts of Manica and Tete provinces, as well as along National Highway 1 in eastern Sofala, but it was largely disorganized and appeared contained by FPLM troops. Meanwhile, Renamo for its part was pleased to have survived this onslaught and of securing a powerful new patron in the form of South Africa. Thanks to *Voz da Africa Livre* broadcasts and the South African pressganging of illegal Mozambique immigrants, some 1,000 new recruits were in the training pipeline that would swell the insurgent ranks to 4,000 and rising.[28] With this recovery and its new source of supplies from South Africa beginning to flow, it would be only a matter of time before Renamo was once again able to return to the offensive.

4. GROWING REGIONAL ENTANGLEMENTS

Even as both Frelimo and Renamo were regrouping and recovering after many months of hard fighting in the aftermath of Zimbabwean independence, Mozambique's neighbors were finding themselves increasingly drawn into the conflict. Pretoria saw in the Renamo insurgency a highly effective tool for not only destabilizing the communist-aligned Frelimo government, but also for curtailing the ANC military threat now emanating from Mozambique and for sending a broader message about the high cost of supporting the anti-apartheid struggle. For Mozambique's black African neighbors the widening conflict was seen as part and parcel of the final phase of the liberation of southern Africa, a struggle that many owed President Machel a huge debt of gratitude. Now it was their turn to assist an embattled Mozambique in its time of need. Thus, as the fighting resumed and intensified, so too would the level of outside intervention. This in turn not only fueled rising levels of violence, but it would also complicate the search for peace.

The South African Factor

The story of the Mozambican war is one that is inescapably intertwined with the regional struggle against apartheid, Pretoria's destabilization efforts against its neighbors, and South Africa's role in the Cold War in Africa. South Africa's timely intervention and the strategic relationship that blossomed between Pretoria and Renamo thus became a crucial factor in shaping the course and intensity of the war. Without this involvement the insurgency would likely never have grown so quickly or expanded so rapidly. Dhlakama's denials to the contrary,[1] Pretoria's direct involvement in the 1980s was indeed the catalyst that made Renamo the military threat that it became to Frelimo.

With the transfer of Renamo's support structure to South Africa, the insurgency entered a new phase that put it on the road to recovery and signaled a significant escalation of the war. After overcoming some initial organizational obstacles and chain of command issues within the South African Defence Force (SADF), an elaborate set of mechanisms was put in place under the Directorate of Special Tasks (DST) within South African military intelligence. Colonel van Niekerk, as officer commanding DST-2 (Eastern Operations), would be in charge of running South African aid to Renamo, known as Operation Altar.[2] This would be a massive undertaking that included providing everything from logistics, training, communications and intelligence, and operational support to the provision of strategic military guidance, the creation of secure rear areas, and most importantly funding. This extensive amount of South African aid was instrumental in facilitating the dramatic expansion of the insurgency from 1982 onward. It also permitted Renamo forces in the field, who were now largely unhindered by logistics restraints, to gain and maintain the battlefield initiative against the Frelimo government well into 1985.

South African Prime Minister P. W. Botha sought to use every tool at his disposal to ensure the survival of the apartheid regime.

The chief priority of both van Niekerk and Dhlakama was rebuilding Renamo's strength and its operational capability in the aftermath of the insurgents' 1980 setbacks by training and equipping a new cadre of guerrilla fighters, as well as creating a robust military supply chain to provide extensive logistics support to Renamo forces inside Mozambique.

Aggressive recruiting—including forced recruitment—and South African-assisted training efforts allowed Renamo to swell its ranks quickly, enabling Dhlakama to put thousands of new guerrilla fighters in the field and renew the fight against Frelimo. The training in South Africa of several hundred recruits at a time at Letaba Ranch included not only weapons handling, marksmanship, and basic guerrilla tactics, but was also designed to identity potential platoon

General Magnus Malan, who also later served as defense minister, was viewed as the most powerful man in South Africa after P. W. Botha.

leaders and those for advanced training. Thus, a small percentage of each class would be selected to attend specialized training in communications, intelligence, medicine, and demolition and explosives, and some 30 to 40 female Renamo soldiers were trained as nurses too.[3] The bulk of the training, however, was done inside Mozambique by rotating SADF recce commando teams. It began in earnest in 1981 with a team under the command of Captain Scott-Donelan deployed to Renamo's Chicarre base in Manica Province and consisted largely of black and white ex-Rhodesian SAS and Selous Scout members, many of whom had previously worked with Renamo.[4] Thanks to these ongoing South African efforts, Dhlakama's force would eventually grow to some 12,000 by early 1984.

Utilizing South Africa's significant airlift capability along with periodic seaborne deliveries by the navy, van Niekerk was able to deliver an estimated 170–180 metric tonnes of war matériel per month to Renamo to sustain its operations.[5] In addition to the routine supply of weapons and ammunition, these shipments also included a substantial amount of non-military items ranging from medical supplies, clothing, and even soap to office supplies, hoes, and seeds. The bulk of the resupply would be done by monthly SAAF C-130 Hercules flying out of Waterkloof airbase outside of Pretoria to predetermined drop zones inside Mozambique,[6] although smaller DC-3 and DC-4 military aircraft were also used as well to supply smaller outlying insurgent bases. In addition to carrying cargo, these smaller aircraft ferried Dhlakama and his staff, senior Renamo commanders, South African VIPs, and specially trained guerrillas into and out of bush landing strips. Largely unreported, the South African Navy aided the resupply effort too by utilizing the 18,980-ton replenishment ship, the SAS *Tafelberg*, and the 2,750-ton hydrological survey ship, the SAS *Protea*. These ships operated clandestinely up and down the coast from Maputo to south of the Zambezi River mouth, although the landing site at Baia McCuluine (Culemine Bay) about 50 miles north of Beira appears to have been the primary landing zone for seaborne deliveries given its close proximity to Renamo's central operating area.[7]

Renamo's military capability was also greatly enhanced by South Africa's provision of a state-of-the-art military communications network that was far superior to anything Frelimo was able to field throughout the war. All company-size Renamo units were equipped with radios, which permitted secure communications between far-flung field commanders and Renamo headquarters, as well with the insurgent rear base in South Africa. In addition, the network provided timely intelligence information on Frelimo troop and aircraft movements passed on from South African listening posts.[8] This assistance provided Dhlakama with a tremendous tactical advantage on the battlefield that Renamo would enjoy almost throughout the entire course of the war and it permitted him and his senior commanders to exercise a high degree of centralized control and coordination over their forces in the field.

Finally, Pretoria sought to use the Renamo insurgency as cover for some of its more high-profile destabilization efforts against Mozambique's economic infrastructure. In late 1981 a joint South African–Renamo force attacked the Pungwe River rail and

By the early 1980s Renamo training camps in South Africa were turning out several thousand trained guerrilla fighters annually.

road bridges northwest of Beira, as well as sabotaging the vital Dona Ana rail bridge over the Zambezi River at Sena. South African recce commandos were also responsible for destroying eight of nine marker buoys in Beira harbor in November 1981 and then followed it up a year later in December 1982 with the destruction of the Zimbabwean fuel depot in the city, resulting in the loss of two months' supply and causing $20 million in damages.[9] Renamo publicly claimed credit for all these attacks, providing Pretoria with plausible deniability.

Over the course of the war the South Africans would brazenly use their one-sided relationship with Renamo to manipulate the insurgency as a tool to advance their own foreign policy and security agenda. Renamo was simply a means to an end. As long as the fighting and the ongoing conflict benefited Pretoria, then it would continue. But once Pretoria had achieved its objectives, Renamo then became expendable.

Gorongosa Airdrop

A typical South African Air Force resupply mission to the Renamo headquarters at Gorongosa in the early 1980s would be a dark-moon sortie involving three to four C-130 Hercules aircraft. Each plane carried 5,500-6,300 pounds of cargo and departed Pretoria's Waterkloof airbase in the late evening hours. The palletized cargo loads, fairly constant from month to month, would include 500 AK-47 assault rifles, over a million rounds of 7.62-mm ammunition, 1,200 60-mm and 600 81-mm mortar bombs, 800 hand grenades, and 400 anti-tank and 300 anti-personnel mines, along with large quantities of explosives, detonators, and timers. In addition to this weaponry, the shipment would often contain medical supplies, field radios and battery packs, uniform clothing, and propaganda material. This latter consisted of Renamo posters and pamphlets, thousands of manila envelopes containing corn, bean, and sorghum seeds, hoes, and consumer goods such as soap, sugar, tobacco, writing materials, and batteries that were intended for distribution to the local population in Renamo-controlled areas.

Flying southeast from Pretoria toward the Durban–St. Lucia area and then swinging far out to sea and northward up the Mozambican Channel, the tight Hercules formations stayed below radar level and flew in complete darkness, using only single quick scans on their radars so as to avoid detection. Usually less than an hour before the drop, the formation would bank left and turned inland over Mozambique for the final approach to the designated drop zone. "We sometimes carried two navigators per aircraft, because we had to be on the ball, flying below hilltop level in the starlight," recalls a former navigator. The guerrillas on the ground used a series of predetermined bonfires in a line, which were lit after a radio call from the aircraft when it was ten minutes out, to visually signal the drop zones, which were constantly changing. "We dropped loads from about 1,000 feet above ground" and "the whole load [normally 15 pallets] went in about three seconds using an extraction parachute. As it crossed the back ramp the aircraft pitched up uncontrollably under the weight shift." The return flight was also at low level back down the Mozambique Channel or on occasion crossing the southeastern Zimbabwean lowveld, touching down at Waterkloof just as the sun was rising.

Although the C-130 pilots and crews now make the missions sound routine, it was anything but given the number of things that could go wrong. As one officer recalls:

The monthly nighttime resupply mission to Gorongosa was a "max effort" using four C-130 aircraft out of Waterkloof. The inward leg down the Mozambique Channel and then turning inland at the mouth of the Save River was uneventful. We made the approach up to the Gorongosa DZ [drop zone] in a line of four, along the main north–south highway and one could see the glow of Beira go by to the right. During the pre-flight briefing in Afrikaans the crews were instructed "*reg uit*" or "right on, continue ahead" for two minutes after their drop before making a right-hand, 180-degree turn for home. The third aircraft, however, misheard the instructions as "*regs uit*" or "turn right and depart the scene" and began an immediate 90-degree turn for two minutes after making his drop. We, in the fourth aircraft, saw the stars go black for a brief second as the 36-ton plane ahead cut directly across in front of us at the same altitude and in total darkness. I still shudder today when I think of it.

Amazingly, no C-130 aircraft were lost that night or during the entire Operation Altar/ Mila resupply missions flown by the South African Air Force from 1981 to 1984.

Source: Adapted from S. Emerson, *The Battle for Mozambique*, pp. 103-105.

The War Enters a New Phase

Now that his South African support infrastructure was in place and men and supplies were flowing into the country, Dhlakama moved in the second half of 1981 to expand Renamo's operational area in central and southern Mozambique and to intensify its activities. With some 4,000 trained guerrillas fighters now under his command, Dhlakama was feeling increasingly confident and optimist about the future. So much so that he was predicting the overthrow of the Machel government by 1985.[10] Renamo units

South African Air Force C-130 transport aircraft were a key cog in Pretoria's supply line to Dhlakama's forces inside Mozambique from 1980 to 1984.

began to re-infiltrate north of the Beira corridor and established small operational bases of about 100–200 men in the northern parts of Manica and Sofala provinces, as well as into southern Tete Province. Most notably and at the strong urging of van Niekerk, Renamo established an operational presence for the first time south of the Save River in Inhambane and Gaza provinces by the end of the year. This would not only facilitate resupply by sea into coastal areas of Inhambane, but shorten Renamo's supply lines to the South African border and create a buffer to counter ANC infiltration through Gaza. Van Niekerk also—unsuccessfully—pushed for Renamo to open a front in Maputo Province and begin an urban terrorism campaign against the capital itself.[11]

Unfortunately for Dhlakama, Pretoria's insistence on a "southern strategy" conflicted with his desire to reassert Renamo's dominance in the central region of the country as a way to put pressure on the Machel government. Moreover, the central provinces were home to Renamo's traditional base of support and where its forces enjoyed a distinct operational advantage, in contrast to the south of the country where Frelimo enjoyed strong popular support and the dry, sparse terrain in Gaza made guerrilla warfare difficult. Thus, as would often happen over the course of the war, Dhlakama would need to find a way to placate his friend "Commander Charlie," while also exercising a degree of operational autonomy over the insurgency. One way to do this and gain favor with Pretoria was for Renamo to disrupt efforts by Frelimo and its SADCC neighbors to make use of alternative transportation routes—such as the Beira corridor's rail and road network—to break their economic dependence on South Africa. Thus began an orchestrated insurgent campaign against central Mozambique's transportation infrastructure: bridges were blown, trains derailed, fuel storage depots and pipelines attacked, and trucks ambushed and burned. National Highway 1 in southern Sofala was singled out for special attention by guerrillas, launching hit-and-run attacks and soon traffic between Beira and Maputo was restricted to vehicles traveling in military convoys during daylight hours.

Just as important, Dhlakama made the decision to relocate his headquarters from Chicarre back to Gorongosa and in early December a 300-man battalion arrived in the Sadjunjira area just to the east of Gorongosa Mountain to establish the new base, which became known as Casa Banana. Symbolically, the guerrillas pledged never to leave the area again, noting that "if we did not stay put, we would never again regain the trust and respect of the local residents."[12] In due course the Casa Banana complex would grow to include an extensive collection of crude buildings housing a command post, communication center, and workshops, as well as primitive housing structures. A rough airstrip was also hacked out of the bush to the east of the base that was able to accommodate DC-3 transports and other small planes.[13] It was from Casa Banana that Dhlakama and his senior commanders would direct a new phase of the insurgency that would bring the war to the very doorstep of the capital itself.

Frelimo was not sitting idly by, but was busy preparing for next round too and ready to take the fight to the insurgents by attacking Renamo's Chicarre base. Since discovering the location of the base in southern Manica Province, Major General Tomé Eduardo had spent months planning Operation Punishment and positioning his forces with the goal

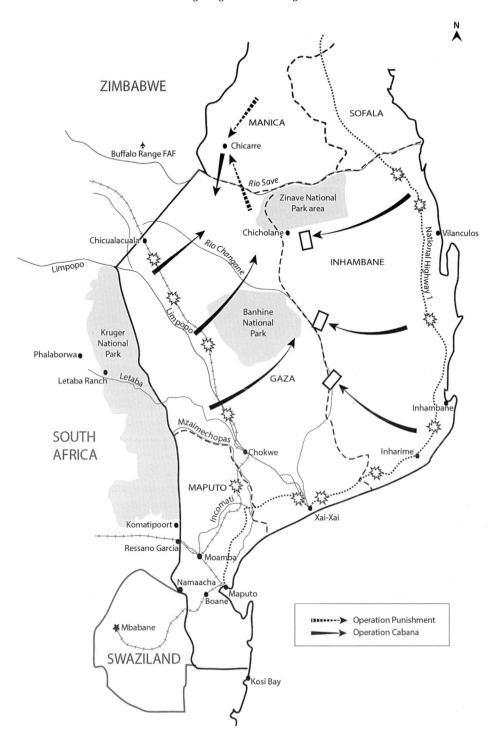

The Southern Front, 1983–1985.

of trapping Dhlakama and finally crushing Renamo. The operation got underway on December 4 and called for a two-pronged infantry assault, supported by air strikes and artillery, on the base. Eduardo's FPLM force of nearly 1,000 men would drive down from the northeast while elements of 2 Brigade, having crossed the Save River, would move in from the south. Once again, the Zimbabwean army would be asked to seal the border to prevent any Renamo forces escaping westward. Air strikes by MiG-17 fighter-bombers went off as scheduled, but from then on nearly everything went wrong. The southern column from 2 Brigade never made it across the Save and Eduardo's force was slow in covering the ground and once at the foot of the mountain ran into stiff resistance. "We found mines had been placed along the approaches to the base," recalled one Frelimo officer, and the enemy was well placed in defensive positions behind large rocks and thus "we lost a lot of people here."[14] Over the course of the next two days the attacking FPLM troops laid siege to the base and rained artillery down on suspected insurgent positions.

After three days of fighting, Chicarre fell to Frelimo. Despite the intense fighting, Renamo suffered only a handful of casualties and nearly all the estimated 500 defenders simply dispersed. (The deployment of numerous Renamo battalions into southern Mozambique and north of the Beira corridor in the months—and even days—prior to

The SAS *Protea* (shown) along with the SAS *Tafelberg* provided thousands of tons in seaborne deliveries to Renamo as part of Operation Altar/ Mila. (Photo Chris Godden)

the Frelimo attack accounted for the relatively small size of the remaining garrison at Chicarre.) The operation was not a total failure, as large quantities of South African military equipment and supplies were captured by Frelimo. However, the biggest prize was not a military one, but the discovery of documents outlining internal Renamo matters, as well as military planning discussions between Dhlakama, van Niekerk, and other South African military personnel that confirmed the large extent of South African involvement and coordination with Renamo.[15]

What was also becoming increasingly clear was that the structure and training of the now 48,000-man Mozambican army was completely ill-suited for fighting a growing insurgency and that the government lacked a comprehensive counterinsurgency strategy. To address the first part of the problem, President Machel in early 1982 called upon its neighbor and longtime Frelimo supporter, Tanzania, to help reorganize and restructure the FPLM. Tanzanian People's Defence Force (TPDF) instructors began replacing Soviet personnel and training was revised to focus on counterinsurgency tactics and operations and away from countering a conventional South African invasion. Machel also replaced provincial governors in the affected provinces with military commanders and veterans of the liberation war were brought back into the army. Mid-year saw the creation of local militias, whose job was to defend villages, health posts, schools, and state farms from Renamo attacks and thus free up the army for offensive operations. Notwithstanding the sense of urgency, it would take some time before these efforts began to show results, time that Frelimo didn't have to lose.

Critically, little progress was made on developing an effective counterinsurgency strategy, although some local commanders apparently experimented with using rural resettlement programs to win the hearts and minds of the peasantry. Unfortunately, the widespread unpopularity of these forced resettlement programs and the new villages' vulnerability to Renamo attacks undercut their potential counterinsurgency benefit. Moreover, Frelimo officials for the most part still refused to believe that any of their social and economic policies might be to blame for fueling the insurgency and instead focused almost entirely on imposing a military solution.

Machel also sought to strengthen and formalize existing security and defense cooperation with Zimbabwe's Robert Mugabe to counter what was emerging as a growing threat to the economic well-being of both countries and their efforts to break free of South Africa's economic stranglehold. For Mugabe this meant helping Frelimo secure the rail, road, and oil pipeline along the Beira corridor, as well as keeping commercial traffic safely flowing along the Tete highway corridor connecting Malawi to Zimbabwe. Following an escalating series of Renamo attacks against the Beira corridor, as well as the high-profile destruction of the Zimbabwean fuel depot in Beira, Mugabe agreed to help Machel by deploying some 1,500–2,000 troops to protect the western half of the Beira corridor in December 1982. Dubbed Operation Lifeline, this action would open the door to full-scale Zimbabwean military intervention—and increasing entanglement in the war—in the years ahead.

While these efforts promised to shore up the government's struggling counterinsurgency effort in the long-term, Renamo forces were expanding their operational reach in

Frelimo troops view captured Renamo weapons and equipment—much of it coming from South Africa. (Photo Centro de Formação Fotografica, Maputo, Mozambique)

both the north and south of the country. Pushing north across the Zambezi River in mid-1982, large groups of guerrillas unleashed their wrath against the country's agricultural heartland, striking towns, factories, and plantations along the river, as well as sabotaging bridges, rail lines, and engaging isolated FPLM outposts. Renamo forces, now reinforced to about 2,000 men, also marched steadily southward along the Inhambane coast and across central Gaza toward the Limpopo River, moving ever closer to the capital. Operating in smaller, lighter-equipped and fast-moving units, they generally avoided contact with numerically superior Frelimo forces, but instead focused their attention on soft targets, cutting lines of communication, and disrupting economic activity. Ambushes, bridge and rail sabotage, and raids on towns, and the looting of shops were the order of the day. Road and rail links in southern Gaza were targeted with the northern part of the rail line from Maputo to Chicualacuala on the Zimbabwean border repeatedly cut. Civilian deaths rose too with indiscriminate attacks on vehicles north of Maputo becoming commonplace, forcing Frelimo to institute a convoy system to safeguard traffic.

To counter the Renamo advance in the south, Frelimo in August 1982 launched Operation Cabana in what would be its largest campaign to date and its first major test of the newly restructured *Forças Armadas de Moçambique* (Armed Forces of Mozambique) or FAM.

An estimated 10,000 men supported by armored vehicles and heavy artillery would be committed over the course of nearly a year in this ambitious undertaking. The plan called for a sealing of the South African border by Frelimo border guards, while the Zimbabwean Army did likewise along its frontier with northern Gaza and southern Manica provinces. Elements of the FAM's 1 Mechanized Brigade along with two other motorized brigades would deploy along the north bank of the Limpopo River and form a defensive line that ran along National Highway 1 through Gaza and Inhambane provinces. Other FAM infantry brigades supported by artillery were then tasked with conducting sweep operations from the Limpopo River valley northward toward the Save River and simultaneously from the Beira corridor southward toward the Save. Meanwhile, newly trained commando teams would launch targeted raids against suspected Renamo base camps to keep the insurgents off balance and on the defensive. The ultimate objective was to drive Renamo forces into a killing zone in the sparse terrain of northern Gaza, where the trapped insurgents would be hammered relentlessly by combined air and ground assaults.

The operation had some initial success in the south because drought conditions caused food shortages for the guerrillas and Frelimo's relocation of villagers exposed Renamo troop movements and made its bases easier to detect. The FAM swept westward across the more remote reaches of southern Inhambane putting the guerrillas to flight and overrunning several Renamo bases, including its main provincial base that yielded more than nine tons of recently airdropped supplies. Similar progress was also made in southern Gaza as Frelimo forces pressed northward. Although few insurgents were killed, large amounts of supplies were captured and Renamo's network of base camps in the south was seriously disrupted. By September FAM units in southern Manica Province launched their phase of the operation with a series of thrusts south toward the Save River, encountering little resistance as the guerrillas gave ground and disbursed.

Despite the apparent inability to inflict significant casualties, Frelimo kept up the pressure on Renamo going into 1983 and not wanting to repeat the mistakes of past offensives. And furthermore, no quarter was given. Heavy artillery was used indiscriminately against suspected insurgent concentrations and villages. Water wells were poisoned to prevent their use. The first public executions of captured guerrillas and collaborators also took place with President Machel warning potential Renamo sympathizers that those who "give information to the bandits will die with the bandits, those who feed the bandits will die with the bandits, [and] those who deal with the bandits will die with the bandits."[16] It all seemed to be paying dividends: producing a sharp decline in insurgent activity in the south in the first half of 1983, disrupting Renamo's logistics network, and allowing Frelimo to re-establish its presence in rural areas previously ceded to Renamo. So much so that Machel would boast that the FAM "had captured 3,500 bandits and thousands more [were] killed or wounded" by October 1983.[17] In reality Renamo escaped largely intact, suffering few casualties, and its losses of weapons and supplies were quickly made good by the South Africans. Moreover, an unforeseen consequence of the offensive was the relocation of large numbers of guerrilla fighters to new areas of the country, such as Maputo Province. The capital was now squarely in the sights of the guerrillas and dark clouds were building.

Despite all President Machel's bravado and public optimism, a day of reckoning was fast approaching for Mozambique in the coming year. The newly reorganized and restructured FAM had proven its mettle in battle and still remained a potent force, but the Frelimo leadership was asking far too much of its military: decisive victory on the battlefield. The events of the past four years had repeatedly demonstrated the FAM's ability to mobilize large number of troops, mount major offensives, overrun Renamo bases, and recapture lost territory. Nonetheless, the FAM's conventional military structure with a reliance on overwhelming firepower, road movement, and extensive logistics and communications support requirements made it ill-suited for the war that it was increasingly forced to fight. Beyond its somewhat questionable ability to bomb Renamo troop concentrations, the air force lacked the necessary lift capability to support a counterinsurgency effort. Tactically, Frelimo forces also lacked any useful counterinsurgency doctrine and instead focused on seizing specific objectives while trying to inflict maximum casualties on the enemy: a goal they seldom achieved. Decentralization of provincial command authority in 1982 had allowed Frelimo to put more men in the field and provide a more localized response to the insurgency, but the increased burden of sustaining this force structure would create long-term problems of equipping, supplying, and maintaining morale.

Zimbabwean troops were first deployed in late 1982 to protect the Beira corridor, but would end carrying much of the offensive burden in central Mozambique by the mid-1980s. (Photo Centro de Formação Fotografica, Maputo, Mozambique)

In contrast, Dhlakama's forces had taken all that Frelimo could throw at them and had not only survived, but they had expanded their geographic reach and were now at the doorstep of Maputo. The training pipeline was churning out thousands of new guerrilla fighters and weapons, ammunition, and supplies were flowing freely from South Africa. Renamo still clearly lacked the capability to contest large-scale FAM offensives directly or fight toe to toe with the enemy, but its forces were well-suited and structured to wage an ongoing war of attrition against Frelimo. Unfortunately, this was a war that Machel and Frelimo could increasingly not afford to fight.

Seven years of war, first at the hands of the Rhodesians and now with Renamo and its South African patron, had left Mozambique in shambles. Thousands of schools, clinics, and shops had been destroyed; rail and road infrastructure were crippled; and business and industry had ground to a halt in some parts of the country. Hundreds of thousands of people had been displaced as a result of years of fighting and growing food shortages. Untold numbers of civilians had also died. War damages in 1982 and 1983 alone likely topped $425 million. South African economic pressure was squeezing Frelimo too—Maputo port traffic was down by 75 percent since 1979 and the combined impact of drought and South African destabilization had cost Mozambique more than $1.85 billion by 1984.[18] The country was $930 million in debt. Machel and Frelimo were at a crossroads. They would make their decision in March 1984 on the banks of the Incomati River with the formal signing of an "Agreement on Non-Aggression and Good Neighbourliness" (better known as the Nkomati Accord) with South Africa.

Pretoria's Economic War on Mozambique

Throughout the 20th century Mozambique's colonial economy was deeply intertwined and heavily dependent on its more powerful neighbor to the southeast, with southern Mozambique becoming a de facto economic appendage of South Africa in the post-World War II period. South Africa was the port of Maputo's biggest client and the largest user of Mozambican rail and port facilities at the time of the country's independence in 1975. It was also the largest employer of Mozambican migrant labor with nearly 120,000 working in South African mines and more than 100,000 laboring in the agricultural sector. And it was the single largest exporter of goods to Mozambique, accounting for more than 20 percent of all imports. This gave South Africa enormous economic leverage over the new post-independence Frelimo government, leverage that Pretoria would not hesitate to exploit for its and Renamo's benefit during the Mozambican war.

Under Portuguese rule Mozambique developed an austere, yet highly profitable rail and port network that not only serviced the colony's exports, but those of its surrounding neighbors as well and provided a critical source of foreign exchange earnings. This was both a blessing and a curse, as it made the international transport services vulnerable to outside pressure by Pretoria. To signal its displeasure with the new Marxist regime and its policies, South African exports through the port of Maputo declined sharply after independence to only 7 percent of the 1973 total by 1988. South African-supported sabotage of the rail network also reduced freight capacity—the Limpopo rail line to southeastern Zimbabwe closed completely in 1984, traffic to Maputo from South Africa and Swaziland fell by 60 percent by 1987, and rail traffic slowed to trickle from the port of Ncala to Malawi by the mid-1980s. Despite the presence of thousands of Zimbabwean troops in central Mozambique, freight traffic along the Beira corridor was only 10 percent of pre-independence levels by the late 1980s. The result was a dramatic fall in foreign exchange surpluses from more than $100 million before independence to less than $1 million in 1985 with Mozambique's annual debt approaching $750 million.

The apartheid government also sought to apply pressure by reducing the number of Mozambican labor migrants working in South Africa, cutting the number of those working in the mines by nearly two-thirds in 1977. Although billed as a way to reduce dependence on foreign workers in the face of political uncertainty, the result was a sharp fall in foreign remittances to the Mozambican treasury. In addition, the lack of migrant labor opportunities left tens of thousands of unemployed and vulnerable youth available to fill the ranks of Renamo's guerrilla army.

Although actions were taken to mitigate the impact of South African economic pressure, such as the creation of the Southern African Development Coordination Conference (SADCC) in April 1980 by Angola, Botswana, Lesotho, Malawi, Mozambique, Swaziland, Tanzania, Zambia, and Zimbabwe as a mechanism for accelerating members' economic growth and reducing their dependence on South Africa, Pretoria's covert support to Renamo throughout much of the 1980s enabled it to undermine Frelimo's efforts to break away from South Africa's economic grip. A report prepared for the Organization of African Unity showed that South African aggression against Mozambique had cost the country at least $10 billion from 1980 to 1984, with annual losses approaching $4 billion by 1985. Throughout the remainder of the war Pretoria would continue to flex its economic muscles to coerce or cajole Frelimo into modifying its behavior with varying degrees of success. In an ironic twist, the Mozambican government would successfully encourage South African economic investment in the country and reconstruction assistance in the aftermath of the war's end in 1992.

Sources: W. Minter, *Apartheid's Contras*, pp. 264-267; P. Johnson and D. Martin, *Destructive Engagement*, pp. 248-252, 271-273.

Above left: Under the Reagan Doctrine the United States sought to aggressively counter Soviet power and influence throughout the Third World by providing overt and covert military assistance to guerrilla movements fighting pro-communist regimes. (Photo White House)

Above right: Prime Minister P. W. Botha sought to burnish South Africa's image as the defender of the West against the "communist onslaught" in southern Africa.

Above left: Angolan rebel leader Jonas Savimbi became the darling of the Reagan administration and his UNITA movement received of millions of dollars in covert American military assistance in the 1980s.

Above right: Afonso Dhlakama proved unable to shed Renamo's tainted historical roots and mold his organization into an effective political movement capable of securing Western support in his battle against Frelimo. (Photo courtesy André Thomashausen)

Angolans and Cubans riding on a BRDM, 1980s: more than 20,000 Cuban troops would pour into Angola to help defend the newly independent Marxist regime against South African- and American-supported rebel groups, such as UNITA.

Thousands of Soviet military advisers and technicians would assist both the MPLA and Frelimo in waging their counterinsurgency campaigns during the 1980s.

Soviet-supplied Mi-24/25 Hind helicopter gunships proved to be a deadly addition to both Luanda's and Maputo's arsenals.

Strengthening air defenses became an essential element of Soviet aid and one that was designed to deter, or at least limit, cross-border air attacks by South African and Rhodesian forces.

The SA-3 ground-to-air missile system provided to both Angola and Mozambique.

The more advanced mobile SA-13 air defense systems provided to MPLA forces would pose a major threat to South African air operations in southern Angola.

Mozambican MiG-17 fighters were used almost exclusively in a ground-attack role against Renamo guerrillas with marginal results.

While Mi-24/25 gunships gave the Mozambican Air Force a powerful firepower advantage, chronic maintenance and logistics problems greatly limited their availability throughout the war. (Photo courtesy Al J. Venter)

Unlike in Mozambique, Pretoria had few qualms about conducting large-scale ground incursions into southern Angola in support of Savimbi's rebel UNITA forces throughout the 1980s.

The South African G5 155-mm artillery piece would play a major role in clashes with government and Cuban forces in Angola. (Photo courtesy Clive Wilsworth)

The high-risk air defense environment over southern Angola and around the Mozambican capital constrained the use of South Africa's most valuable and irreplaceable fighter aircraft. (Photo courtesy Dick Lord)

Mobile air defense units like these successfully shot down a SAAF Impala strike aircraft in 1987 and a Mirage F-1 fighter in 1988 over southern Angola.

Rhodesian forward operating airfield with Alouette III helicopters and a Lynx strike aircraft in the foreground. (Photo Theo Nel)

Selous Scouts preparing for air insertion into hostile territory. (Photo courtesy Craig Fourie)

Aging Hawker-Hunter strike aircraft were the mainstay of close air support for large-scale Rhodesian raids into Mozambique.

South African C-130 transports helped maintain the Rhodesian air bridge to Renamo bases inside Mozambique under Operation Bumper.

By 1977 Rhodesian security forces were given the green light with Operation Dingo to conduct regular strikes against ZANLA bases and transit camps in Mozambique.

Flying columns, often including Eland armored cars, were used by Rhodesian forces to launch ground raids deep into Mozambican territory.

Rhodesian Light Infantry troopers secure captured enemy supplies atop Monte Cassino following the capture of ZANLA's New Chimoio base in early October 1979.

South African Air Force Puma helicopters played a major role during Operation Uric, the largest Rhodesian strike of the war into Gaza Province in early September 1979. (Photo Cliff Webster)

The coup that overthrew the Caetano government in April 1974, known as the Carnation Revolution, signaled an end to more than 450 years of Portuguese rule in Africa.

Arrival of the Commonwealth monitoring force in late December 1979 to oversee the transition from Rhodesia to an independent Zimbabwe in April 1980. (Photo Tom Argyle)

The untimely death of President Samora Machel in October 1986 provoked wholesale changes within Frelimo and the course of the war under the new leadership of Joaquim Chissano.

The release of Nelson Mandela in early 1990 following the rise of F. W. de Klerk to the presidency set the stage for dramatic changes in not only South African domestic politics, but also in its foreign relations.

The ascension of Mikhail Gorbachev to power in March 1990 saw a thawing in US–Soviet relations that would give way to an end of the Cold War.

The fall of Berlin Wall in November 1989; the beginning of the end for communist rule in Eastern Europe.

Boris Yeltsin (with sheet of paper) leads the people of Moscow in resisting communist hardliners' efforts to oust Gorbachev from power in August 1991.

The end of the Soviet Union, December 25, 1991.

False Hope at Nkomati

The Nkomati Accord signed on March 16, 1984 between P. W. Botha and Samora Machel as the leaders of South Africa and Mozambique was supposed to be the prelude to the end of the war. It wasn't. For despite the high costs of "making a deal with the devil," an embattled Machel saw few options for his country and for his leadership of Frelimo. The agreement would buy him time, so he made the ultimate gamble, a gamble that he would lose and one that would cost the Mozambican people another eight years of war and immense suffering and destruction. Peace would eventually come to the country, but Machel would never live to see it.

Discontent had been building for some time within the party and the military over the conduct of the war and the country's downward economic spiral and it finally boiled over in early 1983. Several key members of Frelimo's politburo led by Foreign Minister Joaquim Chissano moved to oust Machel from power, citing the downward slide of the country.[19] Machel's increasingly precarious position spurred him to seek a political solution to the war that would strengthen his traditional base of support within the military—Machel was Frelimo's military commander during the liberation war—and undercut his opponents within the party. Thus began in May an extended period of negotiations between Pretoria and Maputo—and one from which Renamo was pointedly excluded—that would eventually result in a non-aggression agreement. Under the terms of the agreement, both governments agreed to stop aiding armed groups seeking to overthrow the other. It seemed that both Renamo and the ANC had become little more than bargaining chips in a greater game.

Unrelenting South Africa pressure on Frelimo forced President Machel to sign a non-aggression treaty on the banks of the Incomati River in March 1984. (Photo Centro de Formação Fotografica, Maputo, Mozambique)

Celebrating the signing of the Nkomati Accord on March 16, 1984. (Photo Centro de Formação Fotografica, Maputo, Mozambique)

Despite the strong sense of betrayal among other Front Line States, within some quarters of Frelimo, and especially by the ANC, the accord was hailed as a victory for peace by Frelimo. With a binding agreement in hand that prohibited both parties from allowing their territory "to be used as a base, thoroughfare or in any other way by another state, government, foreign military forces, organizations or individuals ... to commit acts of violence, terrorism or aggression against the territorial integrity or political independence of the other,"[20] Machel believed Renamo was finished. Now that Renamo was denied South African assistance the insurgency was as good as done. Just as the loss of Rhodesian support four years earlier had crippled Renamo, many in Frelimo believed that cutting the South African lifeline would be the final nail in the coffin.

What Machel hadn't bargained for was the resilience of the insurgency, as well as the deep divisions within the Botha government over the wisdom of implementing the accord. The skepticism was most pronounced among those closest to Renamo, those who believed the insurgents were on the verge of toppling the Frelimo government. Van Niekerk, who had invested so much in building the insurgency and grooming his relationship with Dhlakama, felt especially betrayed. Why stop now when they were so close to victory? Nonetheless, orders were orders and the military began to grudgingly cut ties to Renamo. The main training camp at Letaba Ranch was closed by April and its rear headquarters in the western Transvaal was shut down in advance of the agreement and transferred to Gorongosa.[21] *Voz da Africa Livre*, which had played such an integral part in the formation of the insurgency, was closed down for good as were the offices of Renamo's political secretariat. SAAF resupply flights were suspended and all recce commandos operating with the insurgents in Mozambique were withdrawn.

South African intelligence, however, would maintain its close ties to Renamo in the post-Nkomati period. DST funding would still continue, albeit at a much reduced level and as South African military stockpiles were used up they were not replenished. Most important, senior intelligence officers arranged prior to the signing of the agreement to provide Dhlakama's forces with an immediate six months' worth of resupply: an estimated 350–400 tons of weapons, ammunition, explosives, and medical supplies.[22] Arrangements were also made to establish a secure communications link between Gorongosa and DST headquarters in Pretoria and a clandestine air resupply network using civilian DC-3 and DC-4 aircraft was put in place.[23] Thus, despite the belief that a new era of peace in southern Africa was at hand, clearly some elements within the South African government and military were hedging their bets by ensuring that their primary tool of destabilization remained intact.

In an apparent signal to Frelimo that it was still a force to be reckoned with, a well-supplied and armed Renamo intensified its activity following the signing of the agreement and was soon active in all ten of the country's provinces, putting government forces on the defensive. Thinly stretched FAM forces were now increasingly confined to protecting major transportation arteries and defending larger towns and district capitals. The security situation inside the country had never been worse with Renamo now averaging 100 attacks per month.[24] Facing the collapse of its budding rapprochement with Frelimo, Pretoria opportunistically offered to mediate an end to the war by strongarming Renamo into accepting a peace agreement. The effort ultimately collapsed in October 1984 following the realization that neither Frelimo nor Renamo was prepared to make meaningful concessions. The negotiations also fatally exposed serious divisions between Renamo's external political wing and the guerrilla leadership inside the country,[25] as well as Pretoria's now diminished leverage over the insurgency in the aftermath of Nkomati. The war would go on.

Backed into a corner, Machel tried to put the best face on the Nkomati Accord in the hope that it would spell the end of South African aid to Renamo. (Photo Centro de Formação Fotografica, Maputo, Mozambique)

5. SHOWDOWN

The failure of the Nkomati Accord to emasculate the insurgent threat, ongoing South African duplicity, and the inconceivability of Frelimo and Renamo achieving any acceptable political solution to the conflict drove both sides to see victory on the battlefield as their sole option. By mid-1985 the momentum was building as each sought to turn the tide decisively in its favor. Apparently the only way peace would come to Mozambique would be through the barrel of the victor's gun. Over the course of the next several years the fighting would rise to a fever pitch as the two sides slugged it out, with the war producing ever-escalating levels of violence and brutality against combatants and civilians alike. The war would also spread directly to and entangle Mozambique's neighbors as never before.

Renamo on the Attack

To demonstrate it was still a force to be reckoned with in the aftermath of Nkomati, Renamo continued to tighten the screws on Frelimo, moving ever closer to the capital with a concerted effort to isolate it. Emphasis was placed on interdicting supply lines and cutting the capital's transportation links to the rest of the country. The rail and road networks north and west of Maputo, including the strategic hub at Magude about 60 miles north of the capital, were repeatedly attacked. The Chicualacuala rail line to Zimbabwe was completely closed down in August 1984 after a spate of damaging attacks and sabotage. National Highway 1 north of Manhica in Maputo Province became an increasingly deadly stretch of road, where traffic came to a standstill at night.

Renamo forces in the south also began operating in larger of groups of 60–80 men and even on occasion up to 200 or more. These larger company-sized formations were used to assault isolated and vulnerable FAM or militia positions with the goal of capturing significant quantities of supplies, weapons, and ammunition. This operational strategy apparently was successful in helping to make up the shortfall in South African supplies, with guerrilla commanders claiming to capture more than 100 tons each month from government forces.[1] To fill its ranks and maintain the heightened operational tempo in the south, Renamo increasingly relied on forced recruitment. Many of these "new recruits" were just children—some reportedly as young as 10 years old—who were abducted from their schools or villages. By some estimates, around 40 percent of Renamo combatants were under the age of 18 at the time of recruitment.[2] Forced to carry away looted goods or captured supplies, the new recruits were marched to remote bush camps near the South African border for several months of rudimentary military training. This and the influx from the now disbanded training camps in South Africa enabled Renamo to field a force in the south of around 2,000 fighters by 1985.

Heavy fighting around Caia on the Zambezi River between 1986 and 1990 destroyed nearly all of the town and much of the surrounding infrastructure. (Photo Centro de Formação Fotografica, Maputo, Mozambique)

Derailed and looted train in Maputo Province. In an effort to isolate the capital, rail lines to South Africa and Swaziland came under constant attack from 1987 onward. (Photo Centro de Formação Fotografica, Maputo, Mozambique)

Even with the increased focus on the southern provinces in 1984 and 1985, Renamo continued to solidify its position in central Mozambique, as well as aggressively push farther north well beyond the Zambezi River. This produced some of the heaviest fighting in the war to date, with the district capital of Maringue in Sofala Province changing hands on a regular basis, the vital railway town of Inhaminga repeatedly raided, and the FAM garrison at Gorongosa town falling under virtual siege. Large-scale clashes also became more commonplace, Renamo claiming to have killed 79 FAM soldiers during an attack on the Pungwe River bridge. According to one estimate, by early 1985 Renamo was responsible for initiating 85 percent of contacts with Frelimo forces.[3]

Impressively too, Dhlakama's forces had pushed hundreds of miles north across Zambezia Province and now small bands were operating in parts of Nampula and Niassa provinces. The important Ncala corridor that consisted of the main road, railway, and communications lines running from the port of Ncala to Malawi fell under attack, as did the key transportation hub at Cuamba in southern Niassa. Road ambushes, the sabotaging of bridges, and raids on small towns, as well as the burning and destruction of plantations and communal villages were the order of the day as Renamo sought to disrupt the country's economic heartland. As it moved even farther north into Cabo Delgado Province Renamo also sought to gain a following among the Makonde people and other longstanding anti-Frelimo elements.

Rural villages and their inhabitants were often the targets of destructive Renamo raids. (Photo Centro de Formação Fotografica, Maputo, Mozambique)

By mid-1985 the Machel government was clearly in trouble. Thanks to South African economic pressure and Renamo's ongoing war of destruction, the Mozambican economy continued its downward spiral. Frelimo forces were spread thin as they were now forced to contest Renamo activity in nearly every province. An inability to stem insurgent advances and persistent supply problems negatively impacted FAM morale. Renamo was feeling increasingly optimist; claiming to have control over about 85 percent of the country's rural population.[4] The Mozambican military was on the ropes. It had few options and was in serious danger of losing the war. So Machel attacked.

Frelimo Counterattacks

Realizing the shifting battlefield fortunes and having gambled and lost on the Nkomati Accords being his salvation, Machel sought to turn the tables on Renamo one more time. By marshalling his best units and most effective commanders in the south, he hoped to roll back the Renamo threat to the capital and inflict a stinging defeat on the insurgents. The plan, however, would leave other parts of the country short of troops and even more weakly defended, a situation Dhlakama was almost certainly to exploit. Machel needed help, so he turned to Zimbabwe.

Although Zimbabwean National Army (ZNA) troops had been helping to guard the oil pipeline and transportation network of the Beira corridor for more than two years, they carefully avoided direct confrontation with Renamo guerrillas. In fact, a *modus vivendi*

Frelimo successfully used massed firepower to dislodge Renamo forces from their bases, but it proved completely ineffective in stemming guerrilla activity.

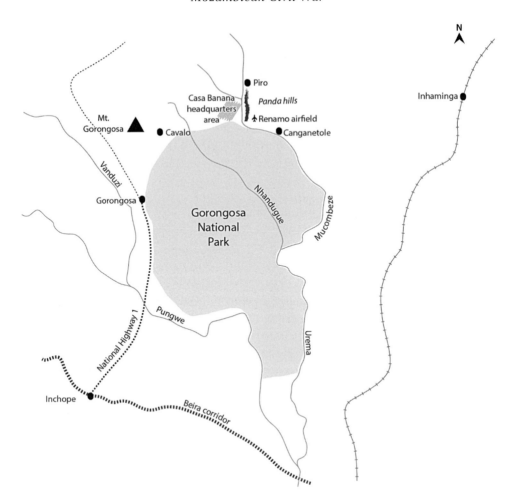

Renamo's Casa Banana Headquarters Complex, August 1985.

had evolved, a live and let live attitude whereby sporadic attacks still continued against the corridor, but commerce and oil still continued to flow uninterrupted. However, the ascendency of Renamo in central Mozambique by mid-1985 meant Dhlakama could now increasingly dictate terms by threatening to shut down this critical economic lifeline to Zimbabwe. Besides, Mugabe owed Machel a huge debt of gratitude for his assistance during the Zimbabwean liberation war and he had a score to settle with Renamo for the movement's role in facilitating Rhodesian attacks on ZANLA forces and bases. Following a June meeting between the two leaders, Mugabe agreed not only to commit more troops to the defense of the Beira corridor, but also to go over onto the offensive against Dhlakama's forces in central Mozambique.[5] Machel's plan was coming together.

The Zimbabwean buildup soon got underway and by early August the Zimbabwean military presence in Mozambique had grown to between 5,000 and 6,000 personnel as it prepared to go on the attack against Renamo. The primary target was Dhlakama's headquarters and Renamo's main supply base at Casa Banana that lay just to the east of Mt. Gorongosa and was estimated to contain some 400–600 personnel. Another 1,000 guerrillas were thought to be spread across the broader Gorongosa area defending the base's outlying areas. The attack, under the codename Operation Grapefruit, was to be spearheaded by the ZNA and supported by Mozambican infantry, artillery, and air assets in the largest joint operation of the war.

The original—and clearly overly ambitious—plan that was developed by senior Zimbabwean and Mozambican generals and their staffs, called for moving thousands of troops in a complex encirclement maneuver to be supported by precisely coordinated air strikes. The reality on the ground, however, quickly forced this plan to be abandoned. Despite the increased ZNA presence, many units were sent to man new defensive positions along the eastern section of the corridor, while ongoing supply and fuel shortages kept FAM units from deploying and grounded the Mozambican air force. In the end, less than 1,000 men and support personnel, along with a handful of aircraft could be tapped for Operation Grapefruit.[6] Moreover, it would be an entirely Zimbabwean operation conducted by units of the Presidential Guard Brigade and 1 Para Group with support from the Air Force of Zimbabwe (AFZ). Nonetheless, confidence was high and the Zimbabweans were eager for their first real taste of combat against Renamo.

Grapefruit got underway in late August with three battalions of the Presidential Guard attempting to move into blocking positions to the west, south, and east of the Casa Banana headquarters. D-Day was set for August 28 when troopers from 1 Para Group would be dropped to the north of the base to drive the enemy into the waiting arms of the Presidential Guard stop groups. Things began to go wrong from the start, however, as the understrength Presidential Guard battalions struggled to get into position in the face of difficult terrain and lack of operational experience. Moreover, there were simply not enough men to effectively block potential Renamo escape routes. Fearful of losing the element of surprise, Lieutenant-Colonel Lionel Dyke as commander of 1 Para Group immediately ordered some 60 of his paratroopers to be dropped directly into the center of Casa Banana and begin the attack. Although vastly outnumbered, the bold assault caught the Renamo defenders off guard, resulting in massive confusion and panic. AFZ Hunter strike aircraft bombed fleeing guerrillas, as the paras formed sweep lines to drive others toward the killing ground in front of the Presidential Guard stop groups. Sporadic fighting continued throughout the day, but the main base complex and the adjoining airstrip were quickly captured and secured by the paratroopers.

The success of the airborne assault, however, was not accompanied by similar success on the ground by the Presidential Guard units. Only one battalion got into its blocking position to the west, while two others became hopelessly lost in the dense bush to the south of the base and remained out of the battle entirely. Not surprisingly, only a small number of Renamo insurgents were killed or wounded; most simply fled in the face of the surprise attack, including Dhlakama and his all of his senior staff. Nonetheless, Frelimo would claim more than 500 Renamo dead and proclaim a major victory. During a September 5 visit to the battlefield, Machel announced that "we have broken the back of

There were never enough Soviet-supplied Mi-8 transport and attack helicopters to go around, nor were they well integrated into a counterinsurgency strategy.

the snake [and] now we are pursuing the head of the snake."[7] While the actual enemy death toll was disappointing, the discovery of key documents detailing ongoing South African support to Renamo (which would come to be known as the "Gorongosa Documents"), as well as the capture of mountains of supplies and weapons, along with the disruption of Renamo's command and control structure, handed President Machel and Frelimo a badly needed psychological victory.

Meanwhile, in the south of the country things were looking up too. A now reinforced FAM was making headway against guerrilla forces there by overrunning several important insurgent bases and disrupting Renamo operations in general. Renamo's main operational base at Xichocoxa in southern Inhambane Province, which supported forces in Gaza, Inhambane, and Maputo provinces, was captured in late September, as was another large base some 30 miles from the capital. These operations helped to relieve the pressure on Maputo and its transportation links. Although the FAM inflicted few casualties in these engagements, it was able to capture or destroy large quantities of supplies and put Renamo to flight, all of which helped boost the confidence and morale of the military. Most important, the capture of Casa Banana and the dislocation of Dhlakama's headquarters along with Renamo's loss of other key bases and irreplaceable supplies during September 1985 not only severely disrupted guerrilla activity and put the insurgents squarely on the defensive in central and southern Mozambique, but it also altered the operational environment for Renamo and Frelimo, now that Zimbabwe was a direct party to the conflict.

MiG-21 fighter aircraft were envisioned as a deterrent to South African cross-border military strikes, but instead ended up being used primarily in a ground-attack role against Renamo.

On the international front there were also positive signs that Machel's overtures to the West were beginning to bear fruit with the Americans. A presidential visit to Washington in September went well—despite hostility from conservative congressional quarters—because both sides saw advantages to improved relations. For Machel it meant the possibility of securing badly needed economic assistance, help in pressing Pretoria to adhere to its Nkomati commitments following the release of the Gorongosa Documents, and preempting fledging efforts in Western countries to provide military aid to Renamo. For President Ronald Reagan it provided an opportunity to wean Mozambique from the Soviet embrace and gain an African ally in peacefully resolving southern African conflicts.

While no direct military assistance was forthcoming from the Americans, the British government of Margaret Thatcher independently sought to spearhead efforts to provide Western security assistance to the Frelimo government. And by February 1986 a British military contingent was training Mozambican soldiers in Zimbabwe, further undermining the role of Soviet and Eastern Bloc military advisers. It would take several more years however, before Mozambique's relations with the West would improve to the point where economic and security assistance could begin to flow freely. Nonetheless, the momentum was on Machel's side.

The British Are Coming

Somewhat surprisingly, it was the British Conservative government of Prime Minister Margret Thatcher that spearheaded Western military and economic assistance to Frelimo from the mid-1980s onward. In a strange Cold War twist in Africa, opposing political ideologies were overcome by a shared personal history and level of individual trust between Prime Minister Thatcher and President Machel going back to the Lancaster House talks over Zimbabwean independence in 1979. Following Machel's 1983 visit to London, British aid to Mozambique began to grow steadily. Much of this aid was directed at improving transportation infrastructure, but the indispensable need to protect and secure key road and rail corridors against Renamo attacks quickly became a priority for London as well. First, through the use of private security companies funded by Her Majesty's Government in 1983, and then through direct British training of Mozambican soldiers in 1986, the level and scope of Whitehall's direct military assistance and involvement in the war expanded.

The responsibility for training from February 1986 onward fell upon the small British training contingent, known as the British Military Advisory Team or BMATT, under the command of then Lieutenant-Colonel Rupert Smith located at Zimbabwe's Nyanga camp in the eastern part of the country. The initial British goal was to train up two full battalions of FAM troops and provide leadership training for the Mozambican officer corps. Despite more than a decade of Soviet, Cuban, and East European military assistance to the Mozambican armed forces, the BMATT advisers found the existing FAM training regimen of poor quality, haphazard, and poorly suited to current counterinsurgency requirements. The British plan called for developing a core of well-trained, motivated, and professionally led units from scratch that would raise the overall quality of the FAM over time.

After overcoming numerous logistical and coordination obstacles, the training effort would steadily grow and by April 1987 the program was providing basic infantry training to some 300 Mozambican recruits every three months. Much of the initial training period was focused on physical conditioning, especially as most recruits arrived in rags, undernourished and suffering from one or more diseases. Then Brigadier-General, Tim Toyne Sewell (commanding officer of BMATT from February 1989 to February 1991) recalls that Mozambican recruits "made excellent soldiers when [they were] well-motivated" and "took great pride in their new clothes and equipment and bonded very quickly with their instructors." Later when Sewell visited these soldiers back in Mozambique, he would frequently see them wearing British cap badges alongside their own FAM insignia with the pride of belonging to the "British Brigade." By late 1989, the Nyanga facility was training 1,000 new recruits every three months.

Economic aid to the embattled Frelimo government was another important component of British engagement, and by 1989 London had committed at least $85 million in financial aid. While not huge in monetary terms, this financial assistance was well-timed and directed at critical infrastructure projects (such as the Ncala and Limpopo rail corridors) providing Maputo with not only economic benefits, but also an important political and psychological boost as well. This financial assistance, in combination with a steady stream of high-level visits of British government officials cumulating in the April 1989 meeting between Thatcher and Chissano in Nyanga would solidify British support for the Frelimo government, and vastly increase Whitehall's diplomatic influence with Maputo.

Source: Adapted from S. Emerson, *The Battle for Mozambique*, pp. 178-180.

A Mozambican Mêlée

The euphoric mood in Maputo and Harare would soon face the realization that Renamo, although suffering setbacks, was far from being defeated. While the bulk of Dhlakama's forces had withdrawn from most of Sofala and Manica provinces in the face of the Zimbabwean offensive, small bands of guerrilla fighters remained behind to harass ZNA and FAM patrols and garrisons, raid supply lines, and continue to strike the Beira corridor. But it was in the north where Renamo sought to turn the tide of battle and prove its staying power. The waning months of 1985 and into 1986 saw a major spike in insurgent attacks along the Zambezi River valley and into southern Tete and Zambezia provinces. The lower Zambezi River towns of Sena, Mutarara, Caia, Mopeia, Marromeu, and Luabo fell to Renamo, as did the important crossroads city of Morrumbala in Zambezia with the Frelimo defenders fleeing in the face of determined insurgent assaults.

The loss of Marromeu, the center of the valley's sugar processing industry, and the rout of the nearly 300-man garrison in early January was especially troubling and spurred the formation of a joint ZNA–FAM operation to retake the town on January 24. Leading Operation Octopus would be Colonel Flint Magama, a politically well-connected, but inexperienced Zimbabwean staff officer. His plan called for a swift air assault to secure the airfield outside the city as a bridgehead for recapturing the city by ZNA troops flown in by the Mozambican air force. Inadequate reconnaissance, logistics and coordination problems, and shortages of aviation fuel hindered the operation and soon the small advance force of paratroopers found itself isolated, under heavy enemy fire, and unable to take the airfield. An overly keen Magama flying in a Mi-25 Hind attack helicopter decided to undertake an aerial reconnaissance of the battlefield and was shot down. Magama and two other ZNA soldiers, along with the three-man Mozambican air crew were killed. Complete disaster was avoided when a hastily assembled relief force from Colonel Dyck's 1 Para Group helped turn the tide, forcing Renamo to retreat from the town and in the

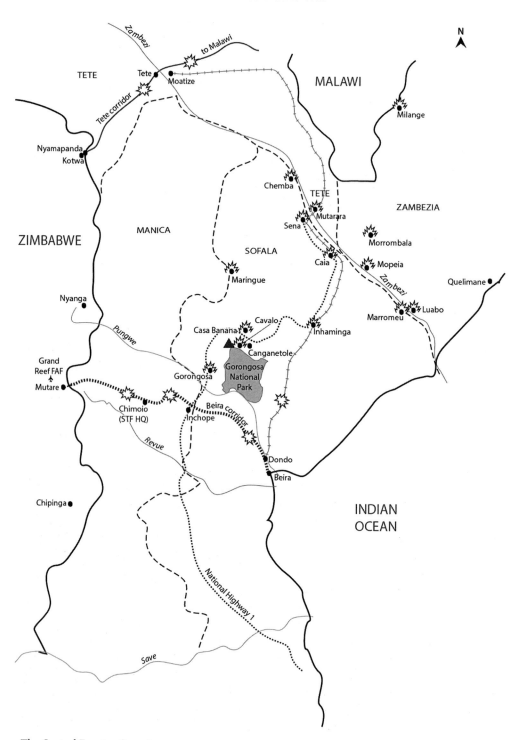

The Central Front, 1985–1987.

process abandoning large quantities of supplies and arms, including tanks and heavy weapons taken previously from the FAM garrison.[8]

While some success was made in checking Renamo operations in the north, increasing numbers of guerrilla fighters were infiltrating back into the Gorongosa area with the onset of the rainy season. On February 14 a Renamo force of some 400 insurgents overran the FAM detachment occupying Casa Banana, capturing large quantities of supplies and heavy weapons. Soon afterward the victorious insurgents were harassing Frelimo's supply lines and laying siege to Cavalo, Gorongosa town, and other FAM positions in the area. The speed of Renamo's recovery and the Frelimo defenders' rapid collapse caught the Zimbabweans completely off guard and it would take nearly two months for them to mount an operation to retake Casa Banana. Following two days of tough fighting in mid-April by nearly 1,000 infantry and airborne troops that were supported by AFZ strike aircraft, Zimbabwean forces were able to dislodge the Renamo defenders. Casa Banana and its adjoining airstrip, as well as Cavalo were now once again in government hands. To avoid a repeat of the capture and loss cycle, the ZNA would maintain a battalion-size presence at the base until the time of 1992 ceasefire.

The second half of the year saw a shift in Harare's operational strategy with the bulk of the ZNA's troops in Mozambique being pulled back to defend the Beira and Tete corridors. Eschewing the large and resource-intense offensives favored by Frelimo, the Zimbabwean counterinsurgency effort would now largely become the responsibility of specialized units, such as 1 Para Group, 1 Commando, and the SAS, or the Special Task Force strike contingent. Operating out of Chimoio or forward airfields in eastern Zimbabwe, these forces relied on mobility and air power to launch ad hoc strikes against Renamo bases and troop concentrations. The goal was to keep Renamo off balance and to prevent it

The FAM constantly struggled to reinvent itself as an effective, mobile light infantry force.

Although both sides launched repeated large-scale offensives, the war would ultimately be decided by the resilience of individual soldiers themselves.

from massing it forces for large-scale offensives. More than 40 of these operations would take place from Tete in the north to Gaza in the south by the end of the war.[9]

Farther afield the situation was not as promising for Frelimo as gains earlier in the year were being reversed by Renamo. All along the Zambezi River from Tete Province to the Mozambican coast, several thousand insurgents were making unprecedented gains, shattering Frelimo's grip, and capturing hundreds of FAM soldiers. By September 1986 Dhlakama's forces were once again in control of a number of important river towns, including Caia and Marromeu, and laying siege to dozens of now isolated garrisons. The intensity of the fighting also precipitated a refugee crisis with thousands of civilians fleeing into neighboring Malawi. The newly captured towns were quickly looted and stripped of anything of value, with Caia, for example, looking "as though vultures had picked clean its carcass."[10] Rather than pin themselves down or expose them to counterattacks and air strikes, Renamo commanders shrewdly established defensive positions outside the now vacant towns.

In Zambezia Province itself, Renamo's "October Offensive" gained it control over nearly all 15 district capitals and had hundreds of fighters pushing deeper into Nampula, Niassa, and Tete provinces. The strategic hub at Milange on the Malawian border was cut off from the rest of Zambezia, forcing some 1,700 FAM soldiers to take refuge in Malawi. It would soon fall to Renamo. By November, an estimated 200,000 Mozambicans had fled the fighting in Tete and Zambezia to become refugees in Malawi and Zimbabwe. While it was speculated that Dhlakama's grand plan was to split the country in two by having Renamo forces control the Zambezi valley and its adjoining districts, this was not the case. For Dhlakama, the critical military weakness of Frelimo was its army's morale, "not training, not equipment, but poor morale."[11] Thus, overrunning or laying siege to FAM garrisons and the insurgents' seeming ability to capture towns at will was a way for Renamo to target this vulnerability and hopefully bring about an implosion of the army.

Although not as desperate, the situation in the south of the country had also deteriorated. Since early 1986 the rail line from Maputo to Swaziland had come under regular attack, while the rail line to Zimbabwe remained closed. Road traffic just north of Maputo was once again subject to bold ambushes by Renamo. In March, guerrillas infiltrated the Matola area on the outskirts of the capital and clashed with FAM forces and the police. Renamo claimed responsibility for a car bombing in a Maputo residential neighbor later in the year, while anti-personnel mines on beaches north of the city injured several people and added to growing security concerns. Likewise, frequent sabotage of powerlines made power outages a regular feature of city life in 1986.

The most climatic event of the year, however, was not a military one, but an unexpected political change. On October 19, 1986 a Soviet-piloted Tupolev 134 aircraft crashed inside South African territory near the Mozambican border after becoming disoriented while attempting a night landing at Maputo's airport. The Mozambican plane was carrying

Frelimo women soldiers mourning the death of President Samora Machel in October 1986.

Large crowds came out in Maputo to watch the funeral procession of their late president, Samora Machel.

President Machel and more than two dozen members of his entourage: Machel and 33 others died in the crash. The confusing and suspicious nature of the crash further strained relations between Maputo and Pretoria and fueled conspiracy theories that would linger for years to come.[12] In Machel's place, Foreign Minister Joaquim Chissano assumed the reins of power amid divisions within Frelimo and growing calls for a negotiated end to the war. Despite some early political struggles, Chissano was able to secure his grip on the party and win the military over to his side. Now all he had to do was win the war against Renamo.

Chissano's War

After consolidating power, Chissano moved quickly to revamp the Mozambican military, address the government's declining fortunes along the Zambezi River and the provinces to the north, and seek to isolate Renamo on the international stage.

In affixing his own stamp on the war, Chissano undertook a series of initiatives to improve the effectiveness of the Mozambican military in early 1987. He replaced Machel's loyal warhorse, Colonel-General Sebastiao Mabote, with the up and coming air force commander, Lieutenant-General Antonio Hama Thai. Likewise, all three service chiefs, along with all current provincial commanders, and the heads of the FAM headquarters directorates were removed to make way for more dynamic leadership. Greater emphasis was placed on promoting combat-experienced officers, developing specialized units (like the Red Beret commandos), increasing the FAM's mobility, and reducing reliance on heavy weapons and mechanized units. The goal was to create a lighter and more specialized force structure specifically designed and equipped for counterinsurgency warfare, one that could go toe to toe with Renamo and turn the tide of the war in Frelimo's favor.

Unfortunately, the challenge of transforming the FAM into an effective counterinsurgency tool was a monumental one. There were some successes. Better British and Tanzanian training programs helped to field stronger units with improved leadership. The selective use of Red Beret commandos against Renamo forces in the south produced some notable accomplishments from late 1987 onward. Likewise, more proficient combat tactics and the discriminating use of heavily equipped forces, such as using mechanized units primarily in the woodland savannahs of Gaza and Inhambane, made some Frelimo operations more effective. Nonetheless, the difficulty of reforming a top-heavy and bureaucratic Soviet-modeled military often proved too much. Poor logistics, chronic maintenance problems, and fuel shortages plagued both the air force and the army. Remote rural FAM outposts were often left to fend for themselves, lacking any resupply for months on end. Attack and transport aircraft often remained grounded, trucks and other vital military equipment sat idle. Moreover, too many FAM and ZNA units were still tied down in defensive missions, thus ceding the initiative to Renamo forces.

But morale did improve and in an effort to reverse Renamo gains and retake key towns and river crossings in central Mozambique, Chissano embarked on a major counteroffensive in early 1987. The operation fell under the command of Lieutenant-General Hama Thai, who established his forward command post at Quelimane. With the support of Zimbabwean forces, the insurgents were ousted from six river towns from Mutarara to Luabo by mid-March and Frelimo was once again in control of the district capital of Morrumbala in western Zambezia Province a month later. The arrival of the first Tanzanian troops, whose number would rise to nearly 3,000 by the end of the year, also helped bolster FAM defenders in eastern Zambezia and put further pressure on guerrilla forces operating there. Initially Renamo put up some stout resistance, but then generally melted away when faced with the overwhelming firepower being assembled against them. Likewise in Tete Province, a ZNA-spearheaded campaign finally pushed the insurgents out of towns in southeastern Tete and along the Malawian border. Smaller and localized operations in the Gorongosa and Maringue districts of northern Sofala Province also were successful in dislodging the insurgents too. Overall, Frelimo claimed to have killed up to 2,000 Renamo insurgents in the fighting.[13]

Renamo for its part continued to move its forces out of harm's way, moving northward up to and across the Licungo River into Nampula Province and even beyond. Once again transportation links and agricultural concerns were priority targets. Sections of the Ncala rail line in Nampula were sabotaged and trains came under regular attack, traffic along the Pemba–Montepuez road was subject to constant guerrilla ambushes. A raid on the rail town of Monapo, about 45 miles southwest of Ncala, killed dozens of civilians and destroyed much of the cashew harvest, while insurgent attacks on northern

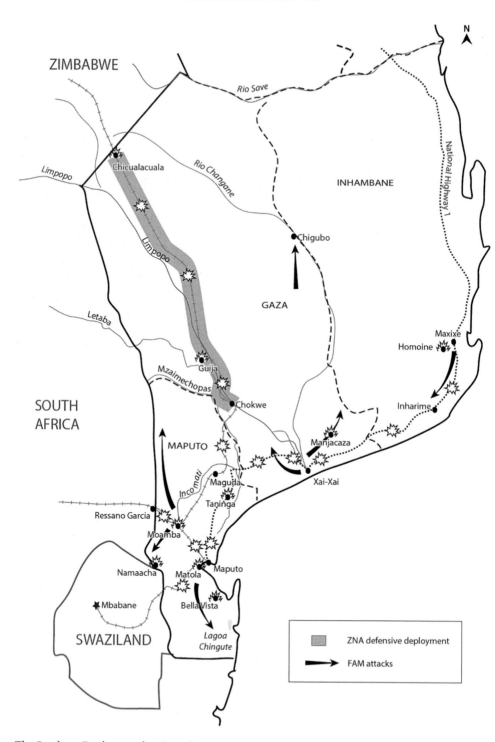

The Southern Battleground, 1987–1989.

Frelimo soldiers inspecting the damage to a village recently raided by Renamo in the south of the country. (Photo Centro de Formação Fotografica, Maputo, Mozambique)

Zambezia's tea-growing region left at least 50 workers dead, tons of tea destroyed, and the processing facilities heavily damaged. Renamo was even claiming major successes in the far north of the country, including overpowering the FAM garrison at Meluco in Cabo Delgado Province and seizing large amounts of supplies and military equipment. During a single week alone in late August 1987, Dhlakama's forces reported engaging in 56 infantry attacks nationwide that destroyed a dozen communal villages and eight military vehicles, while killing 168 FAM and 4 ZNA soldiers at the cost of 29 Renamo dead and 119 wounded.[14]

The fighting had also expanded to neighboring Zimbabawe earlier in June. Dhlakama was seeking retribution against Mugabe for his support of Frelimo by "declaring war on Zimbabwe" and commencing military operations there. Small bands of up to 15 men begin infiltrating northeastern Zimbabwe from Tete Province and were soon joined by other units operating as far south as the mountainous Chipinga area opposite Manica Province. Seeking to incite terror among the Zimbabwean civilian populace, shops and property were looted and burned and agricultural estates attacked and their workers killed. By September Renamo claimed to be operating as far as 30 miles inside Zimbabwe and engaging in three to four major attacks per month. The goal of these attacks, according to a former Renamo general, was to force Harare to defend its own territory and pull troops

Zimbabwean Military Deployments

By late 1982 the government of Robert Mugabe found itself increasingly drawn into the war in Mozambique as Renamo's aggressive strategy of disrupting and destabilizing the Mozambican economy forced Mugabe to intervene to safeguard Zimbabwe's vital transportation and trade routes to the sea that were now under increasing insurgent attack. In the years that followed the Zimbabwean defensive presence in Mozambique would grow and peak at some 7,000–8,000 troops and support personnel, costing the country several million dollars annually in extra defense spending. Their engagement would last up until the end of the war in 1992.

Operation Lifeline

Operation Lifeline began in December 1982 with the initial deployment of some 1,500–2,000 men from the Zimbabwean army's 3 Brigade out of the eastern border city of Mutare. Positioned along the western portion of the Beira corridor—the rail, road, and oil pipeline network that ran from the port of Beira to Mutare— the troops were responsible for deterring Renamo guerrilla attacks against road and rail traffic, as well protecting the corridor's infrastructure, such as bridges, an oil pipeline and its pumping stations, and communication facilities. By 1984 the defensive mission expanded to include protecting the entire length of the corridor, requiring the army to rotate each of its regular 3,000-man brigades into Mozambique for six- to nine-month deployments. A Special Task Force was also established at Chomoio to serve as a headquarters for the rotating brigades with the eventual inclusion of a small air detachment from the Zimbabwean air force to provide support. Lifeline would give way in August 1985 to Operation Grapefruit, which would now include offensive operations against Renamo forces in central Mozambique too.

Operation Cob Web

By mid-1984 Renamo was intensifying its attacks along the 165-mile highway running from Nyamapanda on the Zimbabwean border across Tete Province to Zobue on the Malawian frontier. Vehicles were being ambushed, trucks looted and burned, and the road subject to mining. In response Mozambique, Malawi, and Zimbabwe formed a joint security committee in June to counter the threat, but the Zimbabwean army would carry the burden of protecting the route as part of Operation Cob Web. Elements of the 1st Mechanized Battalion using their Brazilian-made Cascavel armored personnel carriers were dispatched to provide armed escorts and patrol the route. Headquartered at Tete city, the roughly 600-man unit was also charged with protecting the key Tete rail and road bridge over the Zambezi River and responding to Renamo attacks along the road.

Operation Open Way
Rehabilitation of the important rail line running from Chicualacuala on the Zimbabwean frontier to Maputo as part of the Limpopo transportation corridor that had been closed since 1984 began anew in late 1987. At that time the National Railways of Zimbabwe starting moving southward from the border in the face of Renamo harassing raids on its repair crews. To improve security elements of the Zimbabwean army's 4 Brigade was dispatched in 1988 as part of Operation Open Way. Eventually up to 3,000 troops would be deployed in defensive positions, including bunkers and minefields, along the corridor from Chicualacuala to the rail hub at Chokwe in the south. To support the operation a small forward headquarters was established at Chokwe. In addition to the defensive mission of Open Way, small teams of specialized Zimbabwean army units also conducted search-and-destroy operations to keep Renamo forces near the corridor off balance.

out of Mozambique.[15] Over the course of the next two years more than 450 people, including several dozen ZNA soldiers, would die in these attacks.[16]

Mugabe did respond by sending additional troops to the border areas, but beyond the psychological impact and brief boost to Renamo morale, Dhlakama's eastern offensive had little impact on the war in Mozambique. The raids, while annoying and instilling fear in the civilian population, did little real damage to the Zimbabwean economy. They also critically failed to divert large numbers of ZNA troops from Mozambique or force Mugabe to reassess his commitment to Frelimo. In point of fact, the Zimbabwean military presence in Mozambique would expand by the end of 1987 to include operations not only in the central region, but also in the south.

In the second half of 1987, fighting in the south remained concentrated in southern Gaza and Inhambane provinces and throughout much of Maputo Province as the insurgents once more attempted to isolate the capital from the rest of the country. Dhlakama began redeploying some of his forces southward away from central Mozambique earlier in April in response to the FAM–ZNA activity and in preparation for launching his own offensive in the south. *Offensiva Relampago* (Offensive Lightning) got underway in August with Renamo attacks on Frelimo positions to the north and west of the capital. Important rail and road hub towns were not only raided, but completely leveled, this fate befalling Manjacaza in southern Gaza in early August. Rail traffic from South Africa along the Ressano Garcia line and from Swaziland came under heavy attack too. Bridges were blown, trains derailed and looted, and passengers were robbed, killed or taken prisoner. Repeated ambushes of civilian and military convoys from October to December killed hundreds of civilians and soldiers, and left the roads leading in and out of Maputo littered with dozens of burned-out vehicles. One particularly violent ambush took place near Taninga, about 50 miles north of the capital on October 28 that left 278 dead.

The intense fighting in Zambezia Province from 1987 to 1989 produced hundreds of thousands of displaced persons and a refugee crisis in neighboring Malawi. (Photo newscom.com)

This followed the earlier and highly publicized massacre at Homoine in southern Inhambane Province on July 18 that left up to 425 people dead following a Renamo rampage on the town. The war in the south was clearly spinning out of control and thousands of civilians once again found themselves caught in the middle of the fighting.

Ever the diplomat, Chissano adroitly used this escalating brutality against civilians to stoke international condemnation of Renamo and accelerate Mozambique's rapprochement with the West—and the United States in particular—that had begun under Machel. In President Reagan, Chissano found a receptive audience following his October 1987 state visit to Washington. The American goal of luring Mozambique away from the Soviet orbit and promoting democratic and economic reform appeared to mesh well with Chissano's moves to become more non-aligned and abandon hardline socialist policies. Improved bilateral relations also held the promise of opening the tap to badly needed economic and security assistance that Moscow had shown incapable or unwilling to now provide. Moreover, publicized reports of Renamo brutality by international aid organizations and Western diplomats undercut conservative support for the so-called "anti-communist insurgents" in the United States. And Prime Minister Thatcher labeled Renamo one of the "most brutal terrorist movements there is."[17] Although he failed to obtain any commitment for direct military assistance given continuing resistance by

Ronald Reagan greets Joaquim Chissano during the Mozambican president's visit to the White House in October 1987. (Photo White House)

Chissano's 1987 diplomatic offensive. Here he meets with British Prime Minister Margaret Thatcher in London. (Photo newscom.com)

A food truck manages to arrive in Beira, late 1980s. (Photo Chris Cocks)

conservative elements in the U.S. Congress, the United States continued to be the largest donor of humanitarian aid to Mozambique under the Reagan administration. More important, Washington encouraged other Western governments to step up their bilateral efforts to assist the Chissano government and undermine waning Soviet influence.

While Chissano's pursuit of improved relations the West risked alienating more hardline and old guard members in Frelimo and increased the leverage and influence of Western governments over Maputo, they set the stage for an inflow of badly needed Western aid in the years ahead and dashed any remaining hopes Dhlakama had of forging an ideological alliance with Western governments. Political maneuvering aside, both Frelimo and Renamo still believed that ultimately victory would be found on the battlefield by whoever could outlast the other in a test of wills. The time was not yet ready to talk peace.

6. NO END IN SIGHT

In the nearly four years since the signing of the Nkomati Accord, the hoped-for end to the war had not yet come to a country now seemingly locked into a death spiral. Not only had any meaningful peace negotiations failed to materialize, but the intensity of fighting had escalated as both Frelimo and Renamo sought to impose their will through force of arms on the battlefield. Yet the ebb and flow of the war had not produced anything close to military victory for either or, more critically, the motivation to pursue a negotiated end to the conflict. So the fighting and the suffering of the Mozambican people—now compounded by ongoing drought and famine—continued into 1988 with no apparent end in sight.

While events inside Mozambique did not seem to be changing much, the world was on the verge of a massive political upheaval and a transformation of historical proportions— the Cold War was coming to an end. Since the rise of Mikhail Gorbachev to power in 1985, the Soviet Union was undergoing revolutionary socio-economic and political changes; ones that would ultimately spell the end of communism in the Soviet Union and Eastern Europe. The defining characteristic of the post-World War II international order, the East–West competition, was coming to an end with serious implications for Africa's Cold War battlegrounds. Although Soviet influence and military assistance had been steadily declining in Mozambique since Machel's opening to the West, the collapse of the Soviet Union would be a defining watershed for Frelimo and its foreign policy. Securing Western economic and security assistance was now imperative. For Renamo the end of the communist threat in Africa decisively eliminated its ideological raison d'être now that the Cold War struggle was no longer a factor in its conflict with Frelimo. Likewise, with the tap of Pretoria's covert assistance finally running dry and monumental political changes in the offing inside South Africa, Renamo was compelled to reinvent itself as a completely independent and self-sustaining insurgency if it were to survive.

The Slugfest Continues

By 1988 no part of the country was immune from the fighting and destruction of war as Frelimo and Renamo forces continued to exchange body blows. As in past several years the epicenters of the most intense fighting were in Zambezia Province in the north and within a 100-miles radius of the Mozambican capital in the south. Gone however were the traditional patterns of large-scale offensives and counteroffensives followed by periods of rest and regrouping, as the fighting became more continuous year-round. Even more telling, as Frelimo and Renamo forces grew progressively weaker after more than a decade of war, the combat became fiercer as both sought to gain the decisive edge on the battlefield. Try as they might, however, neither could deliver the knockout blow. Nonetheless, no one was quite yet ready to admit it.

Renamo repeatedly sought to isolate Maputo from the rest of the country by targeting the roads leading in and out of the capital. (Photo Centro de Formação Fotografica, Maputo, Mozambique)

The well-troughed landscape north of the Pungwe River across all of Zambezia Province and up to the Ligonha River valley into Nampula Province, as well as along the border areas of southern Malawi continued to see some of the heaviest fighting of the war as towns and villages changed hands on a regular basis. In January Renamo guerrillas destroyed the town of Namacata, on the outskirts of Quelimane, the provincial capital, before retreating. By February they cut the main road from Zambezia into Nampula by occupying Marrapula, just north of the Ligonha River. Other FAM garrisons were besieged or were abandoned after being cut off or running out of supplies, only to be recaptured later before the cycle repeated itself. Attacks on the economic and transportation infrastructure—particularly along the Ncala corridor—also continued unabated, not only disrupting commerce but also hampering humanitarian relief efforts at a time of dramatically rising need. Ambushes and mining of the rail and road links, the sabotage of bridges and communications infrastructure, and destruction of factories, processing plants, and equipment were the order of the day. Thanks, however, in large part to the direct support of Zimbabwean and Tanzanian troops, the FAM was once again able to regain the initiative in the north by mid-year. Frelimo was able to assume control over all major towns along the Zambezi River valley, in southern Tete, and over all of Zambezia Province's district capitals. Most Renamo defenders simply retreated back into the countryside, but Milange on the Malawian frontier was only retaken by the FAM in June following a ground assault by elite Red Beret commandos that was supported by air strikes.

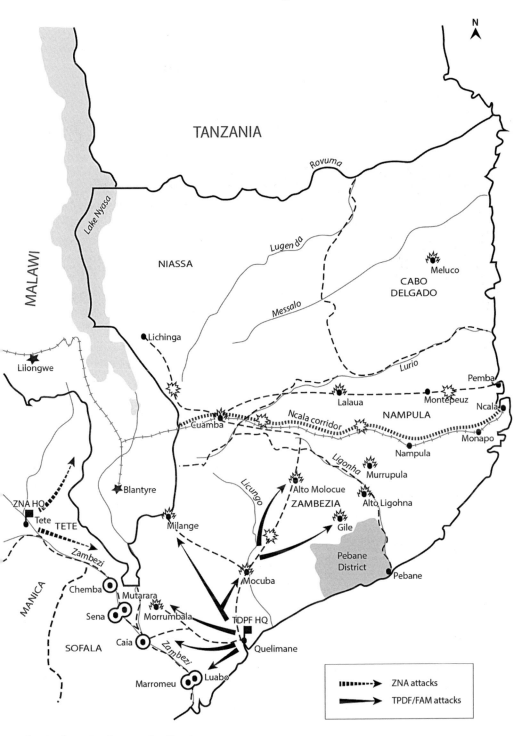

The Northern Battleground, 1987–1990.

During much of the bitter combat, Frelimo often resorted to heavy-handed tactics against Renamo-controlled areas that exacerbated an already desperate situation for civilians caught up in the fighting. Some commanders, such as the Zambezia provincial military commander Lagos Lidimo, were ruthless in implementing scorched-earth policies. Lidimo, a former counter-intelligence chief, vowed to personally execute any of his officers who failed to comply with his orders.[1] Following the recapture of Gile in July, the FAM troops lined up and executed 50 accused Renamo collaborators.[2] Frelimo's Tanzanian allies, however, were highly critical of these tactics, especially the indiscriminate use of air power, claiming it was Mozambican noncombatants who "were being killed in these bombings in a manner amounting to genocide."[3] Not surprisingly, the senior Tanzanian commander in Zambezia noted that his troops "were more popular among the masses than FAM forces," because the latter not only killed civilians but also pilfered relief supplies to make ends meet since they were not adequately fed, paid or clothed.[4]

Renamo was far from blameless too and its forces contributed to depravations of the civilian populace through summary killings, rapes, and massive looting. Civilians were often simply killed on the pretext of being "agents of the enemy" by either Frelimo or Renamo. This heightened violence and the accompanying food shortages soon drove hundreds of thousands of Mozambicans to seek refuge in neighboring Malawi and Zimbabwe, provoking a growing humanitarian crisis. The influx into southern Malawi's Nsanji district was especially telling as it became home to some 220,000 refugees by late 1988. Another estimated 300,000 civilians reportedly fled the fighting in eastern Tete

In the later years of the war attacks on civilians traveling by road in southern Mozambique became increasingly violent and deadly.

Province to seek safety in Malawi and suddenly the country had one of the highest ratios of refugees to population in the world.[5] By 1989 eastern Zimbabwe also became home to more than 100,000 Mozambican refugees fleeing the war.

This massive influx of refugees into Malawi also threatened to upend Chissano's painstaking year-long diplomatic effort to woo President Hastings Banda to his side. The mutual need for both men to secure vital transportation and trade routes through Mozambique against the destabilizing impact of the war led to the signing of a joint Mozambique–Malawi security pact in December 1986. This agreement led to the initial deployment of Malawian troops in April 1987 to help safeguard the western segment of the Ncala rail line and granted FAM troops the right of transit through Malawian territory, as well as the right of hot pursuit into Malawi.[6] Despite this official cooperation, however, some elements within the Banda government remained sympathetic to the insurgents. The country's porous borders facilitated a flourishing trade in looted goods and made Malawi a convenient source of supplies for Renamo troops.[7] Moreover, the country would continue to function quietly as an essential transit point for Renamo officials, serve as base of operations for some private supporters, and provide a critical communication link for Renamo to the outside world up until the end of the war.

Meanwhile, in the far south of the country, nearly all of Maputo Province and the southern parts of Gaza and Inhambane were once again the areas most affected by the fighting. Early 1988 witnessed a spate of Renamo assaults against district capitals: Namaacha and

By the 1990s Frelimo forces increasingly adapted a defensive posture and the war ground on with no end in sight. (Photo Centro de Formação Fotografica, Maputo, Mozambique)

Moamba in western Maputo Province and Guija in Gaza in January and February. Even the country's southernmost district capital of Bella Vista on the Maputo River was raided in mid-February 1988. Road and rail links from Maputo to South Africa and Swaziland came under renewed pressure as Dhlakama sought to tighten the noose around the capital. Commercial and civilian vehicles along these routes were repeatedly ambushed and set alight. One mine blast alone, on New Year's Eve 1987, derailed a train packed with migrant workers from South Africa, killing at least 22 and injuring another seventy-one.[8] Nine Zimbabwe railway workers were killed inside Zimbabwe during an insurgent attack on the Chicualacuala–Maputo rail line in mid-March as the Limpopo corridor north of Chokwe became heavily targeted. Alarmist rumors began to circulate claiming that "up to 5,000" insurgents were massing in southern Inhambane and Maputo province to choke off the capital from the outside world.[9]

To counter Renamo advances and bolster flagging civilian morale in the capital, the FAM intensified its search and destroy operations against Renamo operational bases in the tri-provincial region. Renamo's Gaza provincial base and southern front headquarters was overrun in December 1987 during a combined air and ground assault by the Mozambican air force and Red Beret commandos. General Francisco Paulo Gomes and most of his staff escaped unharmed, but large quantities of supplies were captured or destroyed. Numerous other insurgent bases along the South African border also fell to government forces in the

Remote and isolated FAM outposts were often left to fend for themselves, because of chronic supply shortages.

early months of 1988. The bitter fighting left several hundred dead on both sides. In an apparent effort to boost flagging morale, President Chissano made a tour, in March 1988, of the three war-torn provinces in the south where he reiterated Frelimo's longstanding position that there would be no negotiations with Renamo. By April, Frelimo was claiming it had captured 18 insurgent bases and large quantities of hard-to-replace supplies while killing about 200 during the first quarter of the year. Major success in undermining Renamo morale was touted as well with Maputo reporting that over 1,000 guerrillas had surrendered by July—including several high-profile defections—under its latest amnesty program. This number would rise to over 3,000 by the end of 1988.

The Gersony Report

In April 1988 the results of a U.S. Department of State-funded survey of Mozambican refugees' war experiences by consultant Robert Gersony was released at a critical time in the war with the report proving to be a damning indictment of Renamo's predominant role in civilian mistreatment and deaths, following a spate of highly publicized massacres.

Based on his survey results, Gersony concluded that Renamo guerrillas were directly responsible for at least 100,000 civilian deaths as part of a systematic and coordinated program of violence against civilians. He dispelled the notion that much of the violence was spontaneous or the result of indiscipline. Rather it was an integral part of Renamo strategy to intimidate, control, and to exploit the rural population to provide food and labor. Gersony found that the degree of insurgent control over an area was inversely related to the level and nature of the violence. A weaker insurgent presence was associated with high levels of violence against the Frelimo state and its representatives or designed to instill fear and a sense of insecurity among the populace, while a stronger presence was associated with more limited ritualistic killings to control or cow the people into submission.

While the report had its methodological shortcomings and was severely criticized for its anti-Renamo bias, it came on the heels of the July 1987 Homoine massacre that left 424 dead, as well as several other large-scale insurgent attacks in southern Mozambique that killed more than 350 civilians in late 1987. Thus, the timing of the report couldn't have been worse for Renamo, burdening it with the moniker of a terrorist organization. This international perception, along with Renamo's tainted Rhodesian and South African roots and Chissano's successful diplomatic rapprochement with the West, soon made Renamo an international pariah. More important for the war itself, it effectively ended any hope of Dhlakama gaining external support for his cause beyond some fringe rightwing conservative elements in Europe and the United States. By 1988 Renamo was more isolated and alone than ever before.

War Weariness Sets In

Regardless of the opposing claims as to who was actually winning the war, the fighting had certainly become more ferocious as desperation and exhaustion set in. Frelimo officers operating in the south noted a more aggressive attitude on the part of the Renamo soldiers; it seemed like "no day would go by without us having to fight two to three times a day."[10] For instance, after pushing the insurgents out of their Inharrime District base in southern Inhambane a small FAM stay-behind force suddenly found that rather than flee the area, the guerrillas staged a counterattack in the middle of the night. There was confusion everywhere and "shooting from all directions," recalled a former Frelimo officer that "I thought my own men were shooting at me."[11] In the end the FAM force was forced to abandon the position once again to the insurgents.

Not only was Renamo becoming more aggressive in attacking Frelimo positions, but it was increasingly tenacious in defense. Rather than fleeing FAM assaults on its major bases as in the past, "they tended to resist now when attacked unless there was an overwhelming FAM force" and "sometimes we even had to pull back if not in strength," remembers a Frelimo officer.[12] One attack, on what turned out to be an important Renamo regional supply base, in the Matutuíne District south of the capital, took nearly ten hours to oust the defenders. The attackers lost 27 men, including two officers, while Renamo lost 87 men in the bitter fighting.[13] The huge stockpile of over 1,000 small arms, dozens of boxes of ammunition, and supplies, along with hundreds of head of cattle probably accounted for Renamo's fierce resistance. The withdrawing FAM column came under nearly constant harassing attacks by small guerrilla groups, which were apparently trying to recover at least some of the captured matériel.

Indicative of the times, Renamo was increasingly forced to become a self-sufficient fighting force as the last vestiges of the South African military assistance came to an end in 1988 and it became reliant on captured arms and ammunition to sustain its operations. April's opening of a South African trade office in Maputo was followed by bilateral discussions over security arrangements for safeguarding the Cahora Bassa Dam power lines and in July President Botha promised to cut off—once and for all—any lingering South African aid to Renamo.[14] The spirit if not the letter of Nkomati was being resurrected. While sporadic supplies of mainly food and medicine would trickle into Mozambique up until the end of the war thanks to private and non-official networks in South Africa, Pretoria's support for Renamo was now a thing of the past.

War weariness was also setting in for Frelimo's African allies at a time when Maputo could ill-afford to lose their support. Some 8,000 Zimbabwean troops were now committed to the defense of the Beira and Tete corridors in central Mozambique, as well as to the Limpopo corridor north of Chokwe in Gaza Province. A recently augmented force of up to 1,000 Malawian soldiers was meanwhile protecting traffic along western segment of the Ncala transportation corridor linking Malawi to the sea. At the same time the 3,000-man TPDF contingent in Zambezia Province had proved its worth in stiffing FAM resistance north of the Zambezi River, as well as in spearheading government counteroffensives to retake lost territory over the past two years. Likewise, Zimbabwean search and destroy operations south of the Zambezi helped Frelimo maintain its fragile grip on key towns and river crossings and, importantly, freed up FAM units for offensive operations elsewhere.

Thanks to this direct military assistance, Mozambique's vital rail and road corridors were kept open and functioning and Frelimo continued to maintain its control over all major towns and cities. Nonetheless, the mounting financial and psychological cost of the protracted conflict began to take its toll. Despite Mugabe's pledge to pay any price to secure Zimbabwe's economic lifeline to the sea, the estimated $500,000-per-day price tag, as well as the loss of hundreds of lives and wear and tear on equipment was clearly putting a strain on Zimbabwe's military involvement.[15] While still unwilling to abandon Frelimo to its fate, Harare forces were however increasingly forced to adopt a de facto defensive strategy by late 1988. Gone were the days of large-scale operations. The focus now was on protecting key lines of communication in both central and southern Mozambique, while launching periodic small-scale raids to disrupt Renamo and its operations. The situation for President Nyerere was even more desperate. Given the fragile state of the Tanzanian economy and unable to shoulder the burden of its military deployment, Nyerere began

Renamo made extensive use of child soldiers, some as young as 10 years old, as manpower shortages became chronic. (Photo Paul Moorcraft)

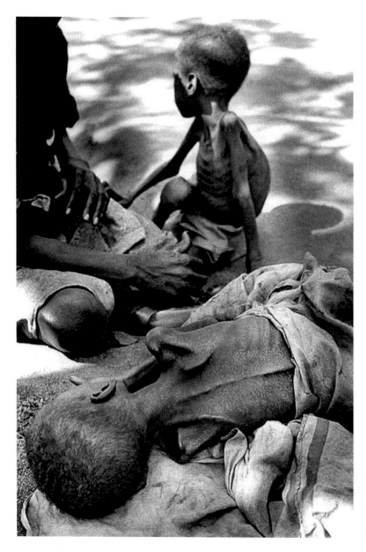

Drought and war-induced famine created vast suffering for the civilian population in the later years of the war.

withdrawing his forces from Zambezia and Nampula provinces in late 1988. By December all TPDF combat troops had been pulled out of Mozambique.

Clearly the war was entering a new period going into 1989. As a consequence of years of bludgeoning each other on the battlefield and declining external assistance, both Frelimo and Renamo had been severely bloodied and weakened. But neither side appeared any closer to military victory or forcing the other to capitulate. Or negotiate. Ultimately, it would take events off the battlefield to finally break this logjam and open the door for a negotiated settlement to the war. Even then it would be a difficult journey filled with many pitfalls along the way.

Peace Talks Amid a Battlefield Stalemate

After years of each side trying to gain the upper hand on the battlefield, most rational observers of the war recognized that a negotiated settlement was the only way to achieve lasting peace in Mozambique. The solution was not to be found through force of arms, but through political compromise at peace talks. A solution was, albeit only reluctantly and quietly, acknowledged by Chissano and Dhlakama as the war dragged on into its twelfth year with the realization that military victory for either was as elusive as ever.

Despite the failure of the South African-engineered peace initiative in the aftermath of the 1984 Nkomati Accord, Protestant and Catholic religious groups in the country worked behind the scenes throughout the second half of the decade to promote a peace dialogue. Neither Frelimo nor Renamo, however, was ready to talk peace seriously as both sides remained convinced of imposing a military solution. Nonetheless, with Chissano's behind-the-scene blessing in late 1987, these church groups assumed a more activist role in brokering direct talks between the warring sides.[16] A key player in this process was the Bishop of Beira, Jaime Gonçalves, who would personally meet with Dhlakama (a nominal Catholic) in Sofala Province in June 1988, establishing a level of trust with Mozambican religious mediators that would pay dividends in the years ahead. The religious community's efforts to promote a peace dialogue became public later that November following the creation of a Peace and Reconciliation Commission headed by the Anglican Bishop of Maputo, Dinis Sengulane.[17] This put increasing pressure on Chissano and Dhlakama to at least privately entertain the notion of indirect talks to avoid being seen as an obstacle to peace. Both leaders would spend the early part of 1989 building support within their respective parties, although hardline elements in Frelimo continued to resist any form of negotiation with Renamo.

A significant breakthrough came in in early August 1989 when Dhlakama flew to Nairobi to join the Renamo delegation discussing Frelimo's Twelve Principles for Dialogue with a high-level Mozambican church delegation that included Gonçalves and Sengulane. The meeting was nearly derailed, however, when a joint ZNA–FAM assault on Renamo's Massala headquarters in northern Sofala Province in mid-July disrupted the delegation's departure plans. Renamo denounced the attack as an attempt by Frelimo hardliners to sabotage the meeting.[18] Chissano denied the allegation, claiming the offensive had been previously planned as part of normal counterinsurgency operations and ultimately Dhlakama arrived on August 3. In response to the Frelimo proposal, Renamo passed along to the church delegation its own Sixteen Points declaration that, among other things, called for Renamo's recognition as a political party on par with Frelimo. This was something Chissano could not accept given Renamo's historical legacy and summarily rejected the document. The talks then stalled despite the intervention of Kenyan and Zimbabwean intermediaries, and would eventually collapse by October. Although ultimately unsuccessful, the talks in Nairobi did create "a whole new dynamic for peace by creating a forum in which both sides could formulate their demands."[19] And like the war itself the newly emergent peace process would be ploddingly slow, deliberate, and be beset by many missteps on both sides. In the meantime the fighting would go on; peace in Mozambique apparently would have to wait.

For the men doing the fighting talk of peace had little relevance. The self-perpetuating cycle of the war—attacks followed by counterattacks, followed by retreats and regrouping only to attack again—showed little sign of changing. The final cutoff of South African aid, however, forced Renamo to alter its operational strategy and tactics. Ammunition and weapon shortages became acute, limiting larger-scale attacks. Renamo's aging South African-supplied communications network began to break down, and with it, its once superior command and control advantage that allow it to quickly redeploy its forces. Likewise, Frelimo forces outside the capital environs and major cities to the north were increasingly on their own, or dependent on Zimbabwean military largess, given the FAM's near complete inability to supply its troops in the field. Food, clothing and ammunition shortages in FAM units were now chronic. The depleted ranks of hardened battle veterans on both sides were now being filled with raw, young and marginally trained recruits as desertion rates soared. Moreover, surviving combat often took a backseat to basic survival as malnutrition and disease dwindled the ranks and capabilities of both armies. Thus, the war was becoming increasingly decentralized and localized, often fought out in bitter isolation.

Increasingly difficult operating conditions in the south of the country—most notably ammunition and food shortages—prevented Dhlakama from deploying sizable numbers of troops as in the past, but the insurgents still tried to maintain the battlefield initiative. Unable to attack the capital directly, General Gomes sought to do the next best thing by creating an ongoing climate of insecurity and fear. The areas to the west and north of Maputo along with the southern districts of Gaza Province continued to experience the heaviest activity with attacks on economic targets, the raiding of garrisons and towns in search of supplies, and the constantly ambushing of vehicular and rail traffic to and from Maputo. Reoccurring Renamo attacks on large sugar plantations, commercial farms, and agricultural processing facilities led to the increased hiring of private security firms to provide protection, train or even lead local militias and paramilitary forces. FAM troops were simply stretched too thin. Likewise, Frelimo forces were unable to halt the spate of deadly attacks on trains and vehicular traffic across Maputo Province. In February 1990 a major Renamo attack on the Ressano Garcia rail line to South Africa left 66 people dead and destroyed a large segment of the track. In May the line was hit again and the train looted.

Renamo's hold on the territory north of the Save River was much stronger than in the south, because declining military effectiveness and growing logistical problems forced Dhlakama to concentrate most of his efforts there. The region's key transportation corridors continued to be subject to Renamo raids, ambushes, and sabotage, although they remained opened thanks to the presence of Zimbabwean and Malawian troops defending them. Maintaining control of the important lower Zambezi River towns from Tambara to Marromeu and the key districts of Zambezia Province was the overriding priority for Frelimo and it was here that it committed the bulk of its efforts. As a result, these areas

The Rise of Naprama

The devastation and displacement following years of war gave rise to a new type of military actor in the late 1980s—independent militia forces led by charismatic leaders with mystical powers. Tired of being repeatedly preyed on by Frelimo and Renamo, these leaders sought to protect their communities and free their people from the ravages of war by forming homegrown militaries to provide an alternative source of security. Or, as the governor of Nampula Province simply put it: "The people tired of war [and] are embracing superstitious beliefs in an attempt to find a way out of the war." These non-affiliated, self-defense forces sprang up all across war-torn regions of the country by the late 1980s, but the most prominent and influential were found north of the Zambezi River. One in particular, Naprama, would end up playing a major role in the closing years of the war.

The Naprama movement traced its roots back to Manuel Antonio in 1989. He was then a 27-year-old traditional healer from the Pebane District of eastern Zambezia Province, who claimed to have died of measles, but after six days in the grave "was revived and told by God to free people" from the ravages of war. Using large ritual, ceremonial gatherings Manuel Antonio "vaccinated" his followers using special medicinal plants and symbolic razor cuts to make them immune to enemy bullets. Thanks to his mystical powers, Manuel Antonio quickly gained a large and loyal following in northern and eastern Zambezia and in March 1990 went on the offensive against Renamo.

Wearing red head bands and armed only with spears and belief in their invulnerability, hundreds of barefoot Naprama warriors marched on Renamo-held towns and bases, singing songs and blowing whistles as they approached. More often than not, the insurgents simply fled at the sight of this mystic army without putting up a fight. By December, Naprama soldiers had overrun some two dozen Renamo strongholds, freeing as many as 200,000 civilians in the process. Even more remarkable, many of these Renamo positions were considered so impregnable that Frelimo forces had repeatedly failed to capture them in the past. At the height of his power in 1991, Manuel Antonio could field some 3,000 core warriors plus tens of thousands of local Naprama militiamen that frequently operated in conjunction with Frelimo troops across much of Zambezia and Nampula and even into southern Cabo Delgado Province.

Despite this success, by 1991 the movement started to move away from its people's army roots. Some elite Naprama troops began wearing uniforms and even arming themselves with captured AK-47s. The role of women became increasingly marginalized too, and many followers abandoned the movement's non-violent tenets. Looting, kidnapping for ransom, and abuses against civilians became increasingly common, and in some instances local commanders would eventually break away to lead roving bands of brigands preying on the civilian populace.

The rapid rise and success of Naprama appeared to surprise and stun Renamo's senior leadership. The poor showing of Dhlakama's troops and the failure to stem the rising Naprama tide threatened to seriously undermine Renamo's strategic position in this critical part of the country. An indication of the seriousness of the situation was the decision by Dhlakama to personally lead a counteroffensive with some of his best fighters against Naprama forces in late 1991. To counter-act Manuel Antonio's mystical power and Naprama's image of invulnerability to bullets, Renamo created its own powerful medicine to make its soldiers immune to the attacks of Naparma warriors. Renamo also unleashed a wave of brutality against Naprama and its supporters. For example, following Renamo's capture of the Naprama-controlled town of Lalaua in Ribáuè District of western Nampula in September 1991, the town was looted and 49 people killed. Many of the dead had their severed heads placed on empty shop shelves by Renamo as a warning to all of the cost of resistance.

The fierce fighting continued throughout the remainder of the year with the reinforced insurgent forces steadily gaining the upper hand. Then the unthinkable happened in early December 1991. Manuel Antonio was killed during a clash with Renamo forces in eastern Zambezia and his body later taken to Quelimane for burial. Following Manuel Antonio's death, the movement fragmented and thus ended its effectiveness as a military force. Most of his followers simply returned to their villages, but some former Naprama soldiers joined Frelimo ranks, while still others turned to banditry.

Sources: C. Nordstrom, *A Different Kind of War Story*, pp. 57-62; J. Weinstein, *Inside Rebellion*, pp. 272-274; *Washington Post*, "Healer in Mozambique Leads Attacks on Rebels," August 4, 1990; *Los Angeles Times*, "Mystery Man Takes Up Mozambique Battle," December 31, 1990.

would bear the brunt of a grinding war of attrition. Smaller guerilla units also oppor-tunistically engaged in launching harassing attacks against FAM positions, raiding and looting villages and small towns, and burning agricultural cooperatives and commercial farms across the region with seeming impunity.

Farther south of the Zambezi valley, old battlefields and ravaged towns across northern Sofala and Manica provinces continued to be the scene of unremitting small-scale fighting throughout 1989 as the Zimbabweans sought to make life difficult for the insurgents by launching periodic air and ground strikes deep into the Renamo-held territory. However, with declining operational capability and sagging morale, beleaguered FAM units south

The harbor at Vilanculos, southern Mozambique, in the late 1980s. (Photo Chris Cocks)

of the Zambezi River became largely confined to static defense and in launching small reactive strikes. By the end of 1989, the FAM was viewed as combat ineffective by its Zimbabwean counterparts.

Frelimo forces still did enjoy some successes. They destroyed numerous insurgent bases, including a very large Renamo logistical base near the South African border in May 1989, putting hundreds of defenders to flight in the process. Moreover, by mid-year FAM troops had successfully retaken control of the central Gaza town of Chigubo, the last remaining district capital held by the insurgents in the province. For the first time since the mid-1980s the insurgents did not control a single district capital in the south.[20] In the north of the country, Chissano's decision to reassign some of his more experienced field commanders to the fight in Zambezia following the departure of the TPDF contingent quickly returned dividends. In one mid-1989 operation a brigade-size FAM force under new leadership overran a major insurgent base in the strategic Alto Ligohna area of Gile District and freed over 1,000 civilians from Renamo control and captured large quantities of badly need supplies from the insurgents.[21]

Going into the new decade the conflict in Mozambique was no closer to resolution. Both Frelimo and Renamo had repeatedly tried and failed to break the other on the battlefield. Both armies were suffering, exhausted, and growing weaker each day, but neither side was willing to call it quits or abandon the use of force. Even an increasingly weak bargaining chip in peace negotiations was better than none at all, especially when both sides had few chips at all to play. The war was now hopelessly stalemated.

7. GLOBAL UPHEAVAL AND THE SEARCH FOR PEACE

Apparently something dramatic would have to change in Mozambique to break the deadlock and somehow push Chissano and Dhlakama to seek a negotiated settlement to the war. But what exactly could that be? As if on cue, the global landscape began to change in ways heretofore unimaginable for both Frelimo and Renamo. And with this change came a histrionic opportunity for finally ending the war in Mozambique. The only question remaining was whether or not Chissano and Dhlakama would boldly seize it.

The Cold War Comes to an End

The summer of 1989 saw building fissures beneath the surface of the Soviet communist bloc finally burst to the surface in earth-shattering fashion. Across Eastern Europe and the republics of the Soviet Union the absolute power of the state and the ruling communist leadership was being challenged as never before. By early November the iconic symbol of communist control—the Berlin Wall—was toppled as people across Eastern Europe celebrated their newfound freedom. While self-determination for Eastern Europe was one thing, Mikhail Gorbachev sought to temper growing demands within the Soviet republics for increased autonomy and even outright independence by proposing the creation of a new Union of Sovereign Soviet Republics at the end of 1990. Under the terms of the so-called Union Treaty, Moscow would grant greater autonomy to the republics, while still maintaining centralized control. It would be too little, too late. An abortive August 1991 coup attempt by reactionary communist elements to reverse the tide of change only served to further inflame popular demands. With Ukraine's declaration of independence on August 24, the writing was on the wall for the Soviet Union, its formal dissolution coming on December 31, 1991 and so too the end of the Cold War.

The rapid unraveling of the Soviet Union presented serious challenges to its African allies, especially those regimes struggling to hold on to power in the face of ongoing insurgencies. Ethiopia's Marxist government of Mengistu Haile Mariam was overthrown in May 1991 following decades of civil war, Angola's civil war raged on, and the Chissano government in Mozambique was holding on for dear life. With the exception of Angola—which had the ability to pay outright for Soviet arms purchases—Moscow's security assistance to the rest of Africa, which was the cornerstone of its relationship, saw a sharp decline by 1990. And although vastly overshadowed by the massive Soviet commitment to Angola, Moscow nonetheless had pumped more than $1 billion worth of arms and equipment into Mozambique by the late 1980s.[1] Despite declining aid levels—falling to some $150 million per year in 1987 from a high of $475 million in 1983[2]—the Soviets and their communist allies continued to maintain a significant military advisory presence

The Berlin Wall, a powerful symbol of communism, comes tumbling down in November 1989.

in the country with an estimated 1,600 Soviet and Cuban advisers.[3] Likewise, hundreds of other Soviet and Eastern Bloc technicians and support personnel provided vital logistics and maintenance assistance to keep the Mozambican army and air force functioning into the 1990s.

While Chissano's turn to the West had already begun to reap significant economic aid benefits by 1990—American assistance alone rising to more than $100 million by 1990[4]—closing the gap in security assistance was proving more challenging. The expansion of the British training program at Nyanga in Zimbabwe in 1989 and London's commitment of $85 million in financial assistance to rehabilitate critical infrastructure, such as the Ncala and Limpopo corridors, were positive signs, but still a drop in the bucket.[5] While improving relations with Lisbon, including a state visit by Prime Minister A. C. Silva in September 1989, presaged budding cooperation on fiscal and economic matters, military assistance was a long way off. Meanwhile, in Washington conservative American political elements and the pro-Renamo lobby continued to block even modest Reagan administration efforts to provide token non-lethal military aid to Frelimo. It seemed Chissano would have to muddle on as best he could as the final days of the Soviet Union came to an end.

Renamo and South Africa were also fast approaching a crossroads as the Soviet Union dissolved and the Cold War came to an end. For Renamo it was a world turned upside down. Dhlakama, who had built his reputation and trumpeted the insurgency as a counterweight to the Soviet-aligned, Marxist one-party state of Frelimo, would now be forced to reinvent himself and his organization. Not only was Renamo more politically, militarily, and diplomatically isolated than ever before, but it had lost its ideological center and raison d'être. Moreover, Chissano's fortuitous rapprochement with the West had steadily moved Mozambique away from its socialist economic roots and his talk of political reforms assuaged Western concerns about the evolution of democracy in the country. Renamo's circle of friends and allies had gotten much smaller and, more important, increasingly irrelevant in the emerging new world order.

For South Africa change was in the air too. The ending of the perceived regional communist threat, the release of Nelson Mandela from prison, and the unbanning of the ANC signaled a new day not only for South Africans, but for Pretoria's relations with its neighbors as well. Rather than work to destabilize Mozambique, President F. W. de Klerk sought to advance common economic development interests and promote regional economic integration. Renamo and the ongoing war was clearly an impediment. Once the ardent patron of Renamo, South Africa now saw peace and stability in Mozambique as a key foreign policy objective. Although clearly unable to play substantive role in any potential peace negotiations given its tainted legacy, the de Klerk government did work actively behind the scenes with the United States to prod Dhlakama to action.

In contrast to these dramatic international and regional shifts, the stalemate on the battlefield also proved to be a catalyst for change. Whatever military leverage Dhlakama thought he had, it was clearly slipping away before his eyes. Dhlakama's army was far weaker and less effective, the fighting was more decentralized and harder to control, and much of the rural civilian population under Renamo control was literally starving to death. The situation was only marginally better for Frelimo. Offensive operations had largely become a thing of the past as years of fighting and a logistics network on the brink of collapse confined the FAM to its bases, major cities and strategic towns or in defense of key lines of communication. Morale was at an all-time low for both sides. Desertions were mounting and widespread and uncontrolled banditry plagued much of the countryside. Maybe now was the time for Chissano and Dhlakama to end the war.

The View from the Front Lines

While often analyzed and discussed in terms of military strategy, the impact of key battles and operations or leadership decisions, war ultimately is fought and often decided—especially in terms of morale—at the individual level of soldier versus soldier and their personal struggle to persevere in the face of extreme adversity. The war in Mozambique was no different. For the soldiers on both sides it was a very personal war, one of triumph and too often tragedy amid the cruelty and suffering of war.

"We mounted an operation [in northern Inhambane Province] to rescue a group of civilians that had been abducted and taken into the interior. After successfully freeing them, we brought supplies and health workers to their village. The bandits attacked one resupply convoy, burning the trucks, looting the supplies, and killing 17 people. We buried them in a mass grave near the ambush site. I never got over that. We were very angry and pursued the attackers, but they got away. A few days later we discovered that the bodies had been unearthed from the grave and their heads cut off. The bodies were lying along the road. And the heads were on stakes like a fence of human heads along the road. It was done to scare the people. It was hard [for me] to believe how a human being could do such a thing."

Frelimo officer recalling a particularly grisly incident in February 1982

"First we were told to guard the pipeline. Now we seem to be fighting the whole war."

Zimbabwean soldier, April 1987

"This operation [in southern Gaza Province] would be a test of our abilities. Not only of silently infiltrating the base undetected, but also of our 'shoot to kill' training after clearly identifying our targets. We learned through a network of spies that the Renamo commander was getting married so we planned to surprise them. We were successful. After a short ten-minute firefight, they broke and ran. The next day, we captured five Renamo spies sent back to check on the status of the camp. We released one to let Renamo know that we were still in control of the base. Later on, we handed over the base to regular FAM troops and withdrew back to our base."

Frelimo commando officer recalling a 1987 special operations attack

"I was sent to Sena [on the Zambezi River] with some 220 men to reinforce a company that was holding the town and protecting the bridge from further damage [the bridge was heavily damaged in 1986 when Renamo blew two spans on either side]. The garrison was badly beaten up by a series of recent attacks. Shortly after my arrival, the besieging Renamo massed a large force and began what was to be a week-long attack against our position, attacking at least twice a day. We were very isolated and supplies arrived late or not at all. With supplies running low on the sixth day, I ordered my officers to the trenches to face the next attack. Then I saw a column of enemy soldiers marching out in the open, only 100–150 meters away. In broad daylight! Out in the open! We opened fire on them, but they kept on marching as we picked them off one by one. They were mostly kids of 14 to 16 years old; something was wrong in their minds, as they were not fearful. It was an unreal experience, like a movie, and I couldn't understand why the enemy was acting this way." [He later learned that it was not uncommon for young Renamo soldiers to consume a fermented mixture of cannabis and alcohol before battle to numb them and "become a machine that does not fear anything."]

Frelimo commander, 1988

"A defector, who had a falling out with the camp's commander, led the Frelimo force to our base [in Maputo Province]. We were caught sleeping. The next thing we knew, enemy infantry was attacking. Then came the tanks [probably armored personnel carriers] and helicopters. It was very fierce. There was confusion everywhere; 42 of us were killed. I was wounded but managed to escape. I thank God for saving me."

Female Renamo soldier remembering a "large battle" in late 1988

"There was a very large warehouse in town that was filled with dried and treated animal skins. Since all the roads in and out of town had been blocked by the enemy for many years, the owner simply left them there. The soldiers were so desperate for food that they began to break into the warehouse and steal the skins. The dried skins were 'cooked' for hours over fires and then eaten. The huge warehouse was emptied in just 15 days."

Frelimo officer defending Caia on the Zambezi River in 1988

It became very difficult to survive [in southern Sofala Province]. There was no rice, no meat or fish. We came back hungry from patrol, but there was no food.

Renamo soldier, late 1989

"We were really suffering. It was hard to find food and sometimes all we had was hot water and wild fruit and nuts to eat."

Renamo soldier in Gaza Province, 1989–1990

"All we could do was hold on [and] hope the war would someday end."

Frelimo soldier fighting in northern Mozambique, 1990

"When will the war end? I was 40 years old and the war was still going on, I had lost my youth. We had no time to build our future—we were just fighting."

Frelimo veteran of the liberation struggle and civil war, 1991

Source: Author interviews, Maputo, Mozambique, 2009–2010.

Talks Gain Momentum

While both parties were still hesitant to engage in direct negotiations, the active involvement of Kenyan President Arap Moi and Zimbabwe's Mugabe (soon to be joined by President Banda of Malawi), along with American encouragement, helped energize the peace process. Important public pronouncements by Chissano in January 1990, over Frelimo's constitutional reforms and plans for free elections in 1991, fueled speculation of a pending Chissano–Dhlakama meeting. Following visits to Washington, London, and

The Renamo delegation to the Rome peace talks in October 1992: Afonso Dhlakama (second from left), Vicente Ululu, and Raul Domingos. (Photo Centro de Formação Fotografica, Maputo, Mozambique)

Lisbon in the spring, Chissano confirmed that his government was ready "to enter into a direct dialogue with Renamo as soon as possible."[6] President Banda's attempt to broker such a face-to-face meeting in Malawi in mid-year, however, failed when Dhlakama appears to have developed cold feet and scuttled the meeting by issuing new preconditions, including the unacceptability of a Zimbabwean mediator role while it still had troops fighting in Mozambique.[7]

Despite this apparent setback, the momentum for peace would be too much to stop now that Chissano and Dhlakama had publicly committed themselves to finding a solution. The only question was what path this process would take. Enter the Italian-based Catholic lay movement, Sant'Egidio, and its prestigious alumnus Archbishop Jaime Gonçalves to provide a way forward along with financial support from the Italian government.[8] Both Frelimo and Renamo quickly agreed to Sant'Egidio's involvement with the talks set to begin July 8, 1990 at the community's compound outside Rome.

Few people would have predicted this breakthrough given the enormous obstacles, ranging from constitutional reforms, elections and political party laws, to ceasefire arrangements, disengagement, demobilization, and the creation of a new national military, which needed to be resolved. Moreover, the lack of mutual trust between Frelimo and Renamo negotiators was palpable. Many times over the course of the next two years the negotiations nearly collapsed or were derailed by seemingly intractable demands from both sides. Nonetheless, the desire for peace amid the fatigue of war and realization that this new opportunity would be short-lived was too powerful to stop the process that had been set in motion.

From the beginning, Renamo's lack of political acumen and its highly centralized decision-making process created difficulties for the negotiations. Despite the best efforts of the Italian facilitators to bolster the Renamo delegation's confidence, "they were fish out of water" and clearly a young and inexperienced Raúl Domingos, as the head of the negotiating team, was overwhelmed, according to one American observer.[9] Dhlakama's request for assistance and advice on political issues was favorably received by the U.S. representative to the talks, as was Dhlakama's request for technical assistance in establishing a secure communication link from Renamo headquarters in Mozambique to Rome.[10] After some initial trepidation, the Frelimo delegation recognized that this type of active Western engagement would be necessary to move the talks forward. Even with this assistance, Renamo's sense of isolationism, and the requirement that Dhlakama sign off on all key decisions would constantly hinder the pace of the talks.

Nonetheless, the first phase of direct talks from early July to December 1990 produced a milestone in ending the war. Slow, but steady progress was made on developing an agenda, resolving the issue of mediation, and building some degree of trust.[11] Frelimo's surprising agreement to open discussions on Renamo's demand for the complete withdrawal of all Zimbabwean troops from Mozambique as a pre-condition to any future ceasefire, however, produced the talk's first major breakthrough. After considerable back and forth, both sides with the help of the church and Italian facilitators formally agreed on December 1 to have all Zimbabwean forces pull back to the Beira and Limpopo corridors. These corridors were defined as being a three-kilometer strip on either side of the road, rail, and pipelines. Renamo agreed to refrain attacking the corridors. The Frelimo delegation leader, Armando Guebuza, provided separate written assurance that "the government did not intend to use the corridors either to support a military escalation or to conduct offensive operations."[12] A newly created, eight-member Joint Verification Commission (JVC) with four members appointed by Frelimo (Congo, France, the Soviet Union, and the United Kingdom) and four appointed by Renamo (Kenya, Portugal, the United States, and Zambia), as well as a military representative from the government and insurgents themselves would monitor compliance of the agreement.

Although problems over implementation and charges of technical violations of the agreement would arise in the ensuring months,[13] by December 28 all the estimated 5,000–6,000 Zimbabwean troops in Mozambique would complete their redeployment to the corridors. The task was simplified by Mugabe's later acknowledgement that only one battalion out of eight ZNA battalions was actually operating out of the corridors by late 1990.[14] Since Harare forces had already assumed a largely defensive posture, this facilitated a winding down of the war and provided a psychological boost to Renamo. According to Domingos, the Zimbabwean pullback and partial ceasefire was the first really positive sign that things were moving forward and that there "was light [at the end of the tunnel]."[15]

The Frelimo delegation to the Rome peace talks in October 1992: Joaquim Chissano (second from right), Amando Guebuza, and Pasocal Mocumbi; Archbishop Jaime Gonçalves is to Chissano's left. (Photo Centro de Formação Fotografica, Maputo, Mozambique)

The December partial ceasefire, however, did not put an end to all fighting. Frelimo and Renamo worked to shore up their existing military positions and consolidate their hold on territory. For the insurgents this meant dealing with the Naprama threat in Zambezia and Nampula provinces. Renamo forces also flexed their muscles in the early months of 1991 by attacking vehicles along the Tete road east of the city leaving dozens dead and temporarily halting emergency food shipments to Malawi. Likewise, small groups of guerrillas in the south under General Gomes continued to down power lines and periodically ambush rail and road traffic around Maputo throughout the year as a constant reminder that the war was far from over.

Nonetheless, change was in the air. In some parts of the country Frelimo and Renamo soldiers were quietly exchanging letters of truce and forming localized ceasefires. It soon became the norm "and we saw that it was impossible to stop that," recalls a former senior Renamo commander.[16] Losing the ability to apply military pressure would seriously erode Renamo's greatest source of leverage in the negotiations: "it motivated us to speed up negotiations in Rome."[17] Many FAM soldiers too were encouraged by the prospect of the peace, because "no one wanted to be the last to die in the war."[18]

The troops in the field, however, would have to wait a little longer as the talks ground on through the remainder of 1991 and into January 1992. Negotiations over thorny political issues such as protocols on new elections laws, the establishment of political parties,

Chissano and Dhlakama embrace. The war is over. (Photo Centro de Formação Fotografica, Maputo, Mozambique)

post-ceasefire modalities, and implementation timetables, still needed to be finalized. Over the course of seven rounds of meetings, Frelimo and Renamo teams with extensive behind-the-scenes help of the official mediators and support from Western governments, hammered out agreements. Much of the time was spent dealing with Renamo's ongoing unhappiness with the JVC's monitoring of December 1990 partial ceasefire violations. Many of these problems and technical violations were the result of the vagueness of the original agreement, and the small size of the JVC team given the enormity of the task required. Despite their frequent threats to void the agreement and walk away, Renamo negotiators apparently saw the greater value of neutralizing their gravest military threat—the Zimbabweans—and the agreement continued to hold.

Outside the formal talks in Rome, private individuals and foreign governments were also working hard to bring about peace in Mozambique. One notable effort involved President Banda's facilitating of the first face-to-face meeting between Dhlakama and Mugabe in Malawi in early January 1992. According to accounts of the meeting, the two men, with very similar backgrounds (guerrilla fighters, Shona-speakers, and Catholic educated), established a rapport and a grudging respect for each other.[19] "You have your dignity and you know what you are fighting for," Mugabe reportedly told Dhlakama at the conclusion of their meeting.[20] Both men left the meeting convinced that peace could be achieved. Mugabe, in fact, would be instrumental in brokering the historic August 1992 meeting between Chissano and Dhlakama in Rome.

Peace at Last

What was to be the final phase of the Rome talks began in June 1992. Both sides settled the details concerning post-war elections, ceasefire arrangements, Renamo demobilization, and the formation of a new integrated national army. The capstone of this effort was the Mugabe-mediated meetings in Rome between Chissano and Dhlakama from August 5–7 that ultimately led to the signing of a declaration of intent to sign a ceasefire agreement by early October and formally end the war. "I knew then [in early August] that peace would really happen," recalls Domingos.[21] On the Sunday morning of October 4, 1992, Chissano and Dhlakama signed the General Peace Agreement (GPA) in Rome. Archbishop Gonçalves was jubilant. The two leaders spoke briefly thanking those who had supported the peace process and expressing hope for the future. "There is no hatred ...," said Dhlakama, as "the armed struggle will be replaced by a political and democratic one."[22] Almost a year after the collapse of the Soviet Union and following twelve rounds of negotiations spanning more than two years, the war was finally over. Peace had come to Mozambique.

The signing of the GPA signaled the official end of the war, but much still needed to be done to ensure success. Renamo faced the huge challenge of moving its troops to designated assembly points. Large-scale desertions plagued many FAM units. Armed banditry

Renamo's participation in the general election from October 27–29, 1994 signaled a new era for both Frelimo and Renamo. Here Dhlakama shows off his voter's card.

by rogue soldiers and opportunistic Frelimo militiamen was rampant. The devastation of war and drought had left large numbers of Mozambicans displaced across the country and in desperate need of emergency food and medical assistance. And the planned United Nations peacekeeping force had yet to take up positions. Nevertheless, the desire for peace was so strong that none of this mattered much to the physically and mentally exhausted Frelimo and Renamo soldiers. When the ceasefire came it was easily complied with "because both sides were fed up with the conflict; we're tired of fighting."[23]

October 4, 1992 remains a date etched forever in these soldiers' memory. The news from Rome [announcing the GPA] "was a big joy to hear," said one Renamo veteran.[24] "It was finally over, now I could go home," remembers another Frelimo soldier.[25] Most combatants were simply happy to be alive and never wanted to go back to military life; "things I saw, I should never have seen at my age," said one former child soldier.[26] In fact, Renamo would have difficulty finding enough suitable volunteers from its ranks to fill its quota of the newly integrated army. They were simply done with military life. Many soldiers returned home in the years ahead to joyous reunions with family members who thought them dead. Others, especially former child soldiers, would struggle to reconnect with their families and fragmented communities in a world void of the violence that had defined their life.

In the years following the end the war, the former enemies would overcome enormous obstacles to peace. Renamo forces were demobilized. A new national military—the Armed Forces for the Defence of Mozambique (FADM)—would be formed. Political parties would be created. Foreign investment returned, and the country began to rebuild. With the country's first ever multiparty legislative and presidential elections on October 27–29, 1994, Mozambique entered a new era. Chissano defeated Dhlakama to capture the presidency, but Renamo was able to win 112 seats to Frelimo's 129 in the new postwar parliament. An estimated 5.4 million people voted in the elections as the ultimate endorsement by the Mozambican people.

NOTES

1. THE COLD WAR IN AFRICA

1. U.S. Government, "National Intelligence Estimate: Soviet Military Policy in the Third World," October 21, 1976, p. 26.
2. A. Venter, *The Zambesi Salient*, p. 270.

2. THE ENEMY OF MY ENEMY

1. *Time*, "The World: Poised Between War and Peace," October 11, 1976.
2. S. Emerson, *The Battle for Mozambique*, p. 30.
3. D. Martin and P. Johnson, *The Struggle for Zimbabwe*, pp. 241-242.
4. Stockholm International Peace Research Institute (SIPRI), SIPRI Arms Transfers Database.
5. J. Cabrita, *The Torturous Road to Democracy*, pp. 146-147.
6. Emerson, p. 38.
7. Cabrita, p. 144.
8. Emerson, p. 39.
9. Author email correspondence with a former Rhodesian instructor, January 2010.
10. Coventry's team at Odzi consisted solely of professional CIO officers with military backgrounds and a few territorial soldiers on rotation. Some accounts incorrectly state that Captain Robert McKenzie (aka Bob McKenna) and his SAS 'A' squadron were involved in training Renamo soldiers at Odzi, but this was not the case. The SAS would later be involved in training recruits inside Mozambique following Renamo's establishment of bases there after August 1979.
11. Cabrita, p. 148.
12. See for example, A. Vines, *Terrorism in Mozambique*, p. 16.
13. This account of events comes from a former Renamo soldier involved in the failed mission. Author interview with former Renamo combatant, Maputo, Mozambique, November 2009.
14. K. Flower, *Serving Secretly*, p. 192.
15. Emerson, p. 42.
16. Cabrita, p. 154.
17. Emerson, p. 42.
18. B. Cole, *The Elite*, p. 188.
19. Martin and Johnson, p. 6.

3. MISSED OPPORTUNITIES

1. More than 80 percent of these would be ZANLA cadres with the remainder coming from the Joshua Nkomo's Zimbabwe People's Revolutionary Army (ZIPRA) that was based in Zambia. The ZANLA number of 10,800 comes from B. Cole, *The Elite*, p. 329.
2. Combined Operations Headquarters, G/4/1, Top Secret, "Short-Term Strategy for Mozambique, 23 March to 23 July 1979," April 3, 1979.
3. Ibid.
4. Author correspondence with a former SAS officer, February 2011.
5. Rhodesian military communications cable, 'A' Squadron to 1 SAS, Top Secret, *Op Blanket Period 261400B to 271400B*, July 27, 1979.

6. Rhodesian military communications cable, Operation Bumper air tasking order, Top Secret, ComOps to Army HQ, November 2, 1979.
7. S. Emerson, *The Battle for Mozambique*, p. 101.
8. P. Johnson and D. Martin, *Destructive Engagement*, p. 13.
9. P. Moorcraft and P. McLaughlin, *The Rhodesian War*, pp. 164-165.
10. Ibid., p. 165.
11. Emerson, p. 56.
12. Moorcraft and McLaughlin, p. 114.
13. P. Geldenhuys, *Rhodesian Air Force Operations*, p. 185.
14. J. Turner, *Continent Ablaze*, p. 132.
15. Rhodesian military communications cable, Top Secret, ComOps to 1 Brigade, 2 Brigade, Selous Scouts, and Rhodesian Light Infantry, 21 December 1979.
16. Rhodesian military communications cable, Top Secret, *Terms of Reference Operation Bumper*, 22 December 1979.
17. K. Flower, *Serving Secretly*, p. 262.
18. J. Cabrita, *The Tortuous Road to Democracy*, p. 163.
19. The original source of the shootout appears to have come from an *Africa Confidential* article in the early 1980s and has been blindly repeated since as fact by multiple authors, including Anders Nilsson, *Unmasking the Bandits: The True Face of the M.N.R* (1990), p. 26; Alex Vines, *RENAMO: Terrorism in Mozambique* (1991), p. 17; and Margaret Hall and Tom Young, *Confronting Leviathan: Mozambique Since Independence* (1997), p.120, as well as in innumerable journal articles. Not to be outdone, the CIA even cited the "shoot out" story as background in its early intelligence analysis of Renamo throughout much of the 1980s.
20. Author interview with former Renamo combatant, Maputo, Mozambique, November 2009; see also Cabrita, p. 163.
21. Moorcraft, p. 260.
22. Author's interview with former Renamo combatant, Maputo, Mozambique, November 2009.
23. Emerson, p. 77.
24. Cabrita, p. 175.
25. Author phone interview with David Scott-Donelan, a former Rhodesian SAS and RLI officer and base commander while serving with the recce commandos, May 20, 2010.
26. Emerson, p. 111.
27. See Cabrita for a very detailed look at the ins and outs of this political maneuvering, pp.182-184.
28. Emerson, p. 81.

4. GROWING REGIONAL ENTANGLEMENTS

1. "The South Africans helped a bit more [than the Rhodesians] but only with small arms. We didn't really need outside help," Dhlakama told a reporter during a 1996 interview. *The Johannesburg Star*, March 13, 1996.
2. Operation Altar was the code name for South African assistance to Renamo from March 1980 until January 1983. After that time it was renamed Operation Mila. Colonel van Niekerk was the officer in charge of both operations.
3. Author interview with David Scott-Donelan, May 20, 2010.
4. Ibid.
5. Author's calculation based on a sampling of Operation Altar/Mila documents. Minter initially came up with a figure of 148 tons/year, but later revised this to 180 tons. See W. Minter, *Apartheid's Contras*, endnote 39, p. 201.

6. Author interview with former South African Air Force officer, November 2009, Johannesburg, South Africa.
7. S. Emerson, *The Battle for Mozambique*, pp. 105-106.
8. South African court documents, *The State vs. Roland Mark Hunter, Derek Andre Hanekom and Patrícia Elizabeth Hanekom*, Schedule B, Section 2.7.1.
9. P. Stiff, *The Silent War*, p. 392.
10. P. Johnson and D. Martin, *Destructive Engagement*, p. 20.
11. Ibid.
12. J. Cabrita, *The Torturous Road to Democracy*, p. 200.
13. Emerson, p. 136.
14. Author interview with former Frelimo combatant, Maputo, Mozambique, November 2009.
15. J. Hanlon, *The Revolution Under Fire*, p. 222; Johnson and Martin, *Destructive Engagement*, p. 19.
16. Hanlon, p. 230.
17. Cabrita, p. 209.
18. Hanlon, p. 255.
19. Cabrita, p. 222.
20. C. Legum, *The Battlefronts of Southern Africa*, p. 324.
21. Emerson, p. 115.
22. Minter, p. 187; Emerson, pp. 106-107.
23. Emerson, pp. 116-117.
24. A. Thomashausen, "The Mozambique National Resistance, p. 32.
25. See A. Vines, *RENAMO: From Democracy to Terrorism*, pp. 22-24 for a detailed discussion of internal Renamo divisions during the negotiations.

5. SHOWDOWN

1. Thomashausen, pp. 34-36.
2. S. Barnes, "The Socio-Economic Reintegration of Demobilised Soldiers in Mozambique."
3. J. Turner, *Continent Ablaze*, p. 141.
4. Turner, p. 141.
5. S. Emerson, *The Battle for Mozambique*, p. 135.
6. Emerson, pp. 137-138.
7. Associated Press, "Claims Troops Crush Mozambican Guerrillas' Base," September 7, 1985.
8. "Report on the Attack on Marromeu," (Harare) February 4, 1986 as cited in N. Mlambo, "Raids on Gorongosa."
9. Ibid.
10. P. Moorcraft, *African Nemesis*, p. 281.
11. Author interview with Afonso Dhlakama, Nampula, Mozambique, May 2012.
12. See *Le Monde diplomatique*, "The mysterious death of Samora Machel," November 2017 for example. Most mainstream accounts, however, point to human error as the culprit for the crash; the same conclusion reached by the multinational board of inquiry that was convened to investigate the cause of the accident.
13. Emerson, p. 155.
14. *Resistência Nacional Moçambicana*, "Balanco do Dia," September 4, 1987. Renamo document in author's possession.
15. Author interview with former Renamo commander, Maputo, Mozambique, May 2012.
16. A. Vines, *From Terrorism to Democracy in Mozambique*, p. 62.
17. A. Vines, *RENAMO: Terrorism in Mozambique*, p. 1.

6. NO END IN SIGHT

1. J. Cabrita, *The Torturous Road to Democracy*, p. 249.
2. A. Vines, *RENAMO: Terrorism in Mozambique*, p. 92.
3. Central Intelligence Organization memorandum, "ZNA Operations in Mozambique," 1987, p. 2.
4. Ibid., p. 3
5. W. Finnegan, *A Complicated War*, p. 143.
6. Vines, endnote 120, p. 141.
7. Author interview with former Renamo combatant, Maputo, Mozambique, October 2010.
8. *The Washington Times*, "RENAMO rebels choke off Mozambique capital," January 7, 1988.
9. Ibid.
10. Author interview with former Frelimo combatant, Maputo, Mozambique, November 2009.
11. Author interview with former Frelimo combatant, Maputo, Mozambique, October 2010.
12. Author interview with former Frelimo combatant, Maputo, Mozambique, November 2009.
13. Ibid.
14. S. Emerson, *The Battle for Mozambique*, p. 120.
15. P. Moorcraft, *Mugabe's War Machine*, p. 125.
16. Vines, p. 121.
17. Ibid.
18. Ibid., p. 122.
19. A. Vines and K. Wilson, "Churches and the Peace Process in Mozambique," p. 140.
20. Emerson, p. 187.
21. Author interview with former Frelimo combatant, Maputo, Mozambique, November 2009.

7. GLOBAL UPHEAVAL AND THE SEARCH FOR PEACE

1. CIA Directorate of Intelligence, Typescript Memorandum, "Soviet Intentions and Activities in Southern Africa," November 26, 1986, p. 2.
2. CIA, Intelligence Assessment, "The Soviets in Mozambique: Is the Payoff Worth the Price?," February 1988, pp. 4, 6.
3. Ibid., p. 3
4. M. Azevedo, "Mozambique and the West," *Conflict Quarterly*, p. 41. It is worth noting that Western economic assistance was already more than three times communist bloc economic aid by 1985.
5. S. Emerson, *The Battle for Mozambique*, pp. 179-180.
6. A. Vines, *From Terrorism to Democracy in Mozambique?*, p. 127.
7. Ibid., p. 128.
8. C. Hume, *Ending Mozambique's War*, p. 32.
9. Author's notes. Comments of former U.S. observer to the Rome talks, October 1998.
10. Hume, pp. 40-42 and p. 47.
11. Ibid., pp. 34-35.
12. Ibid., p. 46.
13. The very narrow definition of the corridors created problems for Frelimo and the Zimbabweans given the existing location of water and power lines, as well as the ZNA logistics base at Chimoio airfield, that were technically "outside" the Beira corridor. This resulted in a constant stream of charges by Renamo to the JVC that the government was in violation of the agreement. See Hume, pp. 47-48 for the challenges facing the JVC early on.
14. K. Chityo and M. Rupiya, "The Zimbabwe Defence Force from 1980–2005," p. 356.
15. Author interview with Raúl Domingos, Maputo, Mozambique, October 2010.
16. Author interview with former Renamo commander, Maputo, Mozambique, October 2010.
17. Ibid.

18. Author interview with former Frelimo combatant, Maputo, Mozambique, October 2010.
19. P. Moorcraft, *Mugabe's War Machine*, p. 127.
20. Author interview with Afonso Dhlakama, Nampula, Mozambique, May 2012.
21. Author interview with Raúl Domingos, Maputo, Mozambique, October 2010.
22. *Radio Mozambique*, October 4, 1992 broadcast as cited in Hume, p. 138.
23. Author interview with former Renamo combatant, Maputo, Mozambique, November 2009.
24. Author interview with former Renamo combatant, Maputo, Mozambique, October 2010.
25. Author interview with former Frelimo combatant, Maputo, Mozambique, November 2009.
26. Ibid.

By 1990, Beira was in a state of chronic decay. (Photo Chris Cocks)

BIBLIOGRAPHY

Azevedo, Mario. "Mozambique and the West: The Search for Common Ground, 1975–1991," *Conflict Quarterly*, Spring 1991.

Barnes, Sam. "The Socio-Economic Reintegration of Demobilized Soldiers in Mozambique." Maputo: UN Development Program, October 1997.

Cabrita, João. *Mozambique: The Tortuous Road to Democracy*. Bassingstoke, UK: Palgrave, 2000.

Central Intelligence Agency. Directorate of Intelligence, Typescript Memorandum. "Soviet Intentions and Activities in Southern Africa." Top Secret. Washington, DC, November 26, 1986.

_____. Intelligence Assessment. "The Soviets in Mozambique: Is the Payoff Worth the Price?" Secret. Washington, DC, February 1988.

Central Intelligence Organization. "ZNA Operations in Mozambique." Top Secret memorandum. Harare, 1987.

Chitiyo, Knox and Martin Rupiya. "Chapter 13: Tracking Zimbabwe's Political History: The Zimbabwean Defence Forces from 1980–2005" in Martin Rupiya (ed.) *Evolutions and Revolutions: A Contemporary History of Militaries in Southern Africa*. Pretoria: Institute for Security Studies, 2005.

Cole, Barbara. *The Elite: The Story of the Rhodesian Special Air Service*. Amanzimtoti, South Africa: Three Knights Publishing, 1985.

Emerson, Stephen. *The Battle for Mozambique: The Frelimo-Renamo Struggle, 1977-1992*. Pinetown, South Africa: 30 Degrees South Publishers, 2013.

Finnegan, William. *A Complicated War: The Harrowing of Mozambique*. Berkeley, CA: University of California Press, 1992.

Flower, Ken. *Serving Secretly: Rhodesia's CIO Chief on the Record*. Alberton, South Africa: Galago Publishing, 1987.

Geldenhuys, Prop. *Rhodesian Air Force Operations, With Airstrike Log*. Durban, South Africa: Just Done Productions, 2007.

Hall, Margaret and Tom Young. *Confronting Leviathan: Mozambique Since Independence*. Athens, OH: Ohio University Press, 1997.

Hanlon, Joseph. *Mozambique: The Revolution Under Fire*. London: Zed Books, Ltd., 1984.

Hume, Cameron. *Ending Mozambique's War: The Role of Mediation and Good Offices*. Washington, DC: U.S. Institute for Peace, 1994.

Johnson, Phyllis and David Martin (eds). *Destructive Engagement: Southern Africa at War*. Harare: Zimbabwe Publishing House, 1986.

Legum, Colin. *The Battlefronts of Southern Africa*. New York: Africana Publishing, 1988.

Los Angeles Times. "Mystery Man Takes Up Mozambique Battle." December 31, 1990.

Martin, David and Phyllis Johnson. *The Struggle for Zimbabwe: The Chimurenga War.* Harare: Zimbabwe Publishing House, 1981.

Minter, William. *Apartheid's Contras: An Inquiry into the Roots of War in Angola and Mozambique.* London: Zed Books, 1994.

Mlambo, Norman. "Raids on Gorongosa: Zimbabwe's Military Involvement in Mozambique, 1982–1992," SACDI Defence Digest, Working Paper No. 3.

Moorcraft, Paul. *African Nemesis: War and Revolution in Southern Africa 1945–2010.* London: Brassey's, 1994.

_____. *Mugabe's War Machine.* Jeppestown, South Africa: Jonathan Ball Publishers, 2012.

Moorcraft, Paul and Peter McLaughlin. *The Rhodesian War: A Military History.* Barnsley, UK: Pen & Sword Military, 2008.

Nordstrom, Carolyn. *A Different Kind of War Story.* Philadelphia: University of Pennsylvania Press, 1997.

Stiff, Peter. *The Silent War: South African Recce Operations, 1969–1994.* Alberton, South Africa: Galago Publishing, 1999.

Stockholm International Peace Research Institute (SIPRI), SIPRI Arms Transfers Database.

The Washington Post. "Healer in Mozambique Leads Attacks on Rebels." August 4, 1990.

The Washington Times. "RENAMO rebels choke off Mozambique capital." January 7, 1988.

Thomashausen, André. "The Mozambique National Resistance" in C. J. Maritz (ed.), *Weerstandsbeweging in Suider-Afrika.* Potchefstroom, South Africa: Potchefstroom Universiteit, 1987.

Time. "The World: Poised Between War and Peace." October 11, 1976.

Turner, John. *Continent Ablaze: The Insurgency Wars in Africa, 1960 to the Present.* London: Arms and Armour Press, 1998.

U.S. Government. "National Intelligence Estimate: Soviet Military Policy in the Third World." Washington, DC, October 21, 1976.

Venter, Al. *The Zambesi Salient: Conflict in Southern Africa.* Cape Town: Timmins, 1974.

Vines, Alex. *RENAMO: From Terrorism to Democracy in Mozambique?.* London: James Currey, 1996.

_____. *RENAMO: Terrorism in Mozambique.* London: James Currey, 1991.

Vines, Alex and Ken Wilson. "Churches and the Peace Process in Mozambique" in Paul Gifford (ed.) *The Christian Churches and the Democratisation of Africa.* New York: Brill, 1995.

Weinstein, Jeremy. *Inside Rebellion: The Politics of Insurgent Violence.* New York: Cambridge University Press, 2007.

Acknowledgements

Special thanks to the dozens of former Frelimo and Renamo soldiers who shared their wartime experiences and personal struggles with me and the Mozambican veterans' association for facilitating those meetings over the years.

I am grateful to Colonel Ricardo Timbe (FADM), Colonel Manuel Mazuze (FADM), and my former student, then Major John Roddy (USA) for all their assistance in facilitating contacts and in helping to make my research trips to Mozambique successful and rewarding.

Joao Cabrita for sharing his time, contacts, and knowledge of events, as well as for assisting me with my field research in Mozambique, including facilitating of my one-on-one interview with Afonso Dhlakama in May 2012.

Thanks to the late Eddy Norris and all the Old Rhodesian Air Force Sods, especially Prop Geldenhuys for his formidable knowledge of Rhodesian air operations and John Reid-Rowland for sharing his photos. To the late John Fairey for his invaluable assistance in gaining access to, and help in deciphering, documents from the Rhodesian Army Association archives then at the British Empire and Commonwealth Museum in Bristol, England.

I extend my deep appreciation to Danny Hartman, Des Robertson, and John Riddick for sharing their experiences and photographs about the early days of Renamo and to Captain David Scott-Donelan and to other former Rhodesian SAS personnel, as well as ex-SADF and ex-SAAF members who asked to remain anonymous.

Special thanks also to Colonel (ret.) Lionel Dyck and other former Zimbabwean National Army officers for sharing their experiences and knowledge about Zimbabwean military operations in Mozambique.

Finally, I would like to highlight the groundbreaking academic and journalistic research on Renamo by the likes of Alex Vines, Paul Moorcraft, Joe Hanlon, Bill Minter, and André Thomashausen.

Index

Stephen Emerson was born in San Diego, California into a U.S. Navy family; his father was a career naval aviator and his mother a former Navy nurse. Steve and his siblings grew up on various Navy bases during the Vietnam War. His father served two combat tours in Vietnam flying both the A-4 Skyhawk and the A-7 Corsair II in 1965 and 1969. Steve is an avid student of Cold War conflicts and military history.

Steve worked as an intelligence analyst covering political-military affairs in Africa and the Middle East before embarking on an academic career. He served as Security Studies Chair at the National Defense University's Africa Center for Strategic Studies and previously as an associate professor of National Security Decision-making at the U.S. Naval War College in Newport, Rhode Island. As the author of more than 100 classified and unclassified publications, Steve has written widely on subjects from American national security affairs and political instability to terrorism, African conflicts, and counter-insurgency. Chief among these are his critical assessment of U.S. counter-terrorism policy in Africa, "The Battle for Africa's Hearts and Minds," and his comprehensive military history of the Mozambican civil war in *The Battle for Mozambique*. He holds a Ph.D. in International Relations/Comparative Politics from the University of Florida and currently resides in Orlando, Florida.

Also by Steve Emerson

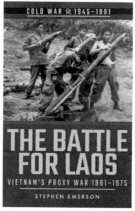